MW00831266

THE FAMILIAR STRANGER

(RE)INTRODUCING THE HOLY SPIRIT TO THOSE IN SEARCH OF AN EXPERIENTIAL SPIRITUALITY

TYLER STATON

BESTSELLING AUTHOR OF
PRAYING LIKE MONKS, LIVING LIKE FOOLS

NELSON
BOOKS

An Imprint of Thomas Nelson

The Familiar Stranger
Copyright © 2025 by Tyler Staton

All rights reserved. No portion of this book may be reproduced, stored in a retrieval system, or transmitted in any form or by any means—electronic, mechanical, photocopy, recording, scanning, or other—except for brief quotations in critical reviews or articles, without the prior written permission of the publisher.

Published in Nashville, Tennessee, by Nelson Books, an imprint of Thomas Nelson. Nelson Books and Thomas Nelson are registered trademarks of HarperCollins Christian Publishing, Inc.

Published in association with the literary agency of Wolgemuth & Wilson.

Thomas Nelson titles may be purchased in bulk for educational, business, fundraising, or sales promotional use. For information, please email SpecialMarkets@ThomasNelson.com.

Unless otherwise noted, Scripture quotations are taken from The Holy Bible, New International Version®, NIV®. Copyright © 1973, 1978, 1984, 2011 by Biblica, Inc.® Used by permission of Zondervan. All rights reserved worldwide. www.Zondervan.com. The "NIV" and "New International Version" are trademarks registered in the United States Patent and Trademark Office by Biblica, Inc.®

Scripture quotations marked ESV are taken from the ESV® Bible (The Holy Bible, English Standard Version®). Copyright © 2001 by Crossway, a publishing ministry of Good News Publishers. Used by permission. All rights reserved.

All emphasis in Scripture quotations is added by the author.

Any internet addresses, phone numbers, or company or product information printed in this book are offered as a resource and are not intended in any way to be or to imply an endorsement by Thomas Nelson, nor does Thomas Nelson vouch for the existence, content, or services of these sites, phone numbers, companies, or products beyond the life of this book.

Library of Congress Cataloging-in-Publication Data

Names: Staton, Tyler, 1987- author.
Title: The familiar stranger : (re)introducing the Holy Spirit to those in search of an experiential spirituality / by Tyler Staton.
Description: Nashville : Thomas Nelson, 2024. | Summary: "Christians today are hungry for authentic spiritual experiences, yet all too often they don't have the knowledge of or relationship with the Holy Spirit that is the key to a fully alive spirituality. In The Familiar Stranger, pastor and author Tyler Staton draws on Scripture, tradition, and spiritual practices to help you step into a genuine relationship with the Holy Spirit"-- Provided by publisher.
Identifiers: LCCN 2024034325 (print) | LCCN 2024034326 (ebook) | ISBN 9781400247707 (hardcover) | ISBN 9781400247813 (ebook)
Subjects: LCSH: Holy Spirit. | Spirituality. | Christian life.
Classification: LCC BT121.3 .S728 2024 (print) | LCC BT121.3 (ebook) | DDC 231/.3--dc23/ eng/20240904
LC record available at https://lccn.loc.gov/2024034325
LC ebook record available at https://lccn.loc.gov/2024034326

Printed in the United States of America

24 25 26 27 28 LBC 5 4 3 2 1

For Hank
Carry the Fire

AUTHOR'S NOTE

EVERY ACCOUNT IN THIS BOOK is written entirely based on true, firsthand experience, according to memory. However, names and identifying details have been changed where appropriate to protect the individuals' privacy.

To serve as pastor in the life of another is an astounding privilege. It is my sincere intention and effort to honor those I've been privileged to companion on the long, winding journey back home. Their stories are the real gift within this book; incarnating the divine, cosmic message in a human body and fallen world turns the rumor of hope into a relatable invitation.

To those whose eyes, like mine, have widened in wonder or welled with tears, those who have awed and grieved, celebrated and suffered alongside me: thank you. Without your stories, this book would be stuck in lofty, detached theory. Your life, broken open, allows others to see their story in yours, your life a living invitation echoing to their own.

INTRODUCTION

PEOPLE SPILLED OUT of restaurants and bars, talking and laughing. A young couple slung heavy laundry totes across their backs and lugged them toward their apartment building. Cars circled, impatiently looking for street parking, and cyclists buzzed past, aggressively ringing their bells. It was nearly 10:00 p.m. Only New York is this raucous on an ordinary Monday night in February. The snow flurries had just begun to fall, and I delighted in their delicate magic drifting to the sidewalk as I strolled and mumbled another prayer of sincere longing under my breath. I kept asking, seeking, hoping for the life of the Spirit rumored on the pages of Scripture, but to this point at least, that life was nothing more than an ancient rumor.

This Monday night prayer walk had become a ritual of mine. I settled with a cozy herbal tea into my typical booth at the quiet café on my block and cracked open my reading, which was always some combination of New Testament narrative and ancient writings. I'd become fascinated by stories of long-ago saints: desert fathers and mothers working miracles of healing for seekers willing to make the pilgrimage, revivals in the heart of the city in which whole prisons repented in a single night, words of prophecy that softened the hardest hearts—hearts that even the most eloquent sermon could never crack. I'd read stories that made me want to believe that every syllable of the Bible was livable. Then I'd pace around the city asking to experience that very presence and power, to become a vessel overflowing with God's living and active Spirit, to find myself among a community to whom such expressions grew from ancient rumor to everyday expectation.

This prayer ritual wasn't born from longing alone, though, but crisis—a quiet, subtle crisis that eventually erupted.

———

I'd just celebrated my twenty-eighth birthday. I was the lead pastor of a church plant in a corner of Brooklyn, New York, where the church attendance figure was 0.01 percent, meaning that if you combined every Christian church of any persuasion—Catholic, evangelical, mainline Protestant, and whatever other variety you might come up with—and measured their combined weekly attendance against the population of our neighborhood, you'd see that just one in a thousand people chose to spend their Sunday morning singing hymns under the glow of stained glass. Brooklyn's overpriced brunches had two-hour waits. Every apartment had an occupant keeping the shades drawn, nursing a hangover. But the church? Ghost town. A couple thousand years earlier, the apostle Paul triumphantly declared the church a visible representation of "the manifold wisdom of God."[1] If he was right about that, my neighbors didn't seem to notice.

The point is that this area was hard soil, a tough place to plant new seeds and see them grow. And that's precisely what made Oaks Church Brooklyn such an anomaly. Two years in we were healthy—financially stable, steadily growing attendance, baptizing and discipling and serving. Everything was going great on paper.

There was this one nagging issue, though. I kept on reading the New Testament. I just couldn't shake the honest realization that the experience rumored about on the pages of Acts was much different from my own. Even though the apostles faced plenty of persecution, trials, and conflicts, they seemed to carry the burden of leading the early church lightly. But I felt I was carrying the weight of the world. They seemed like they were having the adventure of a lifetime. I was stressed and exhausted. They were stewarding teeming life. I was stewarding finances and attendance figures.

Everything was going great on paper, but I was longing for more than a story on paper. I wanted a lived story. How could I rip this life off the pages of Scripture and discover it here and now—in this place, among these people? I'd barely made it two years into this pastor gig and was already facing a quiet crisis. Everything was glistening on the surface, but I carried a holy discontent within.

Not long after starting my Monday-night prayer walks, my wife, Kirsten, found me weeping alone in the living room on a Tuesday morning.

"Tyler, are you okay?" she asked.

"I'm not sure," I replied, once I could get words out. "Weeping" is probably too polite a word for what I was doing. "Wailing" is a better word for it. I was crying like I hadn't cried since I was a little boy who got too gymnastic for my athletic prowess on the backyard swingset.

Just a few minutes earlier, I'd been preparing to walk out the apartment door and head to the church to lead a staff meeting. Then I'd suddenly, profoundly broken. Tears poured out of me like a dam held back for far too long.

What had brought me to this point? It was true that I'd been dealt a series of pastoral disappointments recently, with the latest leaving me feeling abandoned by someone I trusted. Completely blindsided.

But that wasn't what had knocked me prostrate. That was just the final straw—the one that broke the camel's back. Something deeper was behind my tears that morning. It was the increasing distance between the wonder and freedom that had started me on this journey with Jesus and the increasing weight I'd picked up along the way—weight I was never meant to carry on my own.

RUMOR TO REALITY

One of the breakthrough insights of famed Swiss psychologist Carl Jung was his definition of psychological health. To paraphrase, Jung observed that everyone—every last one of us—has a gap between our perceived self and our actual self. There's a gap between my perception of myself (who I think I am, how I think I come across, how I think others see me), and reality (who I really am, how I really come across, and how others actually see me). Psychological health, according to Jung, is narrowing the gap between my perceived self and my actual self as much as possible.[2]

That's true for me. And it's true for you. Kinda scary, huh?

Of course, this gap between perceived and actual self is much easier to see in others. We are all painfully aware of the varying degrees of self-delusion our coworkers, friends, and family members carry within them. But even though that same delusion is present within us, we find it difficult to see.

I'd argue spiritual health is a lot like that. Spiritual health is closing the gap between biblical rumor and actual life as narrowly as possible. Spiritual maturity is narrowing the gap between Kingdom promise and daily grind; between what I believe in my head and what I know in my heart, my emotions, and my bones; between the core beliefs I recite in creeds and sing in worship anthems and the core beliefs I live day in and day out. Spiritual health means that inevitable gap between the story on the page and the story of my life narrows and narrows like a door creaking shut on a dark room until there's barely a blade of light left.

The Holy Spirit is the experiential agent of the Trinitarian God, narrowing the gap between biblical promise and everyday experience and leading to greater spiritual health and maturity.

Quiet crisis, loud crisis, or a combination of the two—everyone who attempts to follow Jesus without a deep, rich understanding of and relationship with the indwelling person, presence, and power of the Holy Spirit will one day be confronted by the gap—maybe the troublingly wide gap—between biblical rumor and actual life.

A SUNDAY MORNING IN LONDON

I became fascinated by the Anglican renewal that swept through England in the 1980s and early '90s. John Wimber (the de facto founder of the Vineyard movement in the US, a So-Cal–born family of charismatic churches) ironically had a much more profound influence on the church in the UK than the church in his own country. It started with a preaching tour at a number of traditional Anglican parishes in the English countryside. The Spirit moved so profoundly that signs and wonders broke out, and dog-collar-wearing, smells-and-bells priests were experiencing miracles as a regular phenomenon. A unique charismatic expression grew up that held tradition and new life in tension: the contemplative and charismatic living together under one roof. These churches may have been a fumbling mess in many ways, but they were alive in the same way the Acts church was alive. That was the word on the street, anyway.

In early 2016, I boarded a plane on a journey to see for myself. When my flight touched down in London, I was full of hope that maybe I'd glimpse some of what I'd been asking for on all those Monday night prayer walks.

I figured that if God were really to speak personally and profoundly to me, I had to be spiritually prepared. I needed to see the sun rise and spend several hours in prayer and achieve some kind of inner state of utter transcendence. So when I peeled my severely jet-lagged self out of bed the morning after arriving, that's exactly what I had in mind.

Instead I lived one of those mornings where everything goes horribly wrong. I went jogging through Hyde Park, got lost, and remained calm until I ended up in a bathroom emergency situation in a foreign land. Eventually I found my way back to my Airbnb, but by the time I was showered and once again out the door, I discovered that the local coffee shop opened late on Sunday mornings, and I was out of time to achieve the Zen state I had planned. I walked to the first of three churches I planned to visit that day, frustrated and uncaffeinated, muttering a quick, defeated prayer as I hustled down the sidewalk: "Lord, I've come all this way out of hunger to know the power of the Holy Spirit. Show me today how to live in the power of your Holy Spirit."

The worship gathering I attended was entirely underwhelming. The crowd was sparse (turns out it was a holiday weekend). I was a stranger, a first-time visitor, and they were doing everything they could to sign me up for all their groups, which was a bit off-putting. The pastor got up to preach and announced the title of his sermon: What Does the Holy Spirit Do?

I wasn't moved by the teaching in the slightest. He'd manuscripted every word and delivered it with a staggering lack of charisma, but he closed with an altar call of sorts—an invitation for anyone who wanted more of the Holy Spirit to come to the front. I thought, *Well, I've already crossed an ocean, so might as well walk a few more steps.*

As I stood there with my eyes closed and hands open, waiting for someone to pray for me, a hand landed on my shoulder—not to pray for me but to awaken me. The pastor with the mediocre, uninspiring sermon was shaking me. "Hey, open your eyes. Come with me."

He proceeded to escort me around the room with him while he ministered to people, telling me what to do: "Lay your hand on her shoulder. Now pray blessing. Wait, listen. Do you have any sense from God come to mind, any thought at all? Okay great, pray it over her."

Eventually the altar area cleared out. I asked the pastor, "Why'd you do that?"

"Do what?" He looked confused.

"Why'd you take me around with you?" I responded. "Why tell me to pray for people, show me what to do? You've never met me before. I could've been nuts."

"Yeah, good point," he said, like this possibility was honestly just occurring to him. "It's just that, as I was making my way through the people responding, I saw you. Then I heard the Lord whisper to me, 'Here's a man filled with the Holy Spirit who has no idea how to live in the power of the Holy Spirit. Show him,' So I did."

It was the direct answer to the exasperated prayer I'd muttered earlier that morning on the sidewalk.

And that was it for me—when the story began to come off the page.

———

It was the combination of a long, slow, quiet crisis and the hunger awakened by a taste of the Spirit's power in London that left me wandering New York City, mumbling prayers on Monday nights and asking God for one simple thing: to show me and teach me the ministry of his Holy Spirit.

"I want that. God, I want to know you in every way I see in Scripture, to lead like they did in Acts, to steward the miraculous, to live that kind of life. I want to know the presence and power of your Spirit, but I'm not even sure where to start."

Not long after I hit that breaking point, weeping in my living room, God answered my prayers, and the years since have been the ride of my life. I started not just reading a biblical story but living one. And you know what? The burden is light, the adventure unpredictable, the presence and power real—and I'm having the time of my life. That combination of crisis and hunger has turned out to be the most potent accelerant in my spiritual life to date.

SALT ON YOUR LIPS

Saint Augustine is credited with praying, "Lord, you have put salt on our lips that we may thirst for you." That's what this book is—salt on your lips that you may thirst for living water.

When it comes to the Holy Spirit, in my pastoral experience I've encountered three categories of people: the thirsty, the suspicious, and the uninformed.

Some of you are thirsty for more of God, longing for any and every way you might experience his presence and power. However, it is not only possible but tragically common to have the right desire without a biblical foundation for that desire. To the thirsty, I want to dig you a biblical well to satisfy that thirst. I hope that in these pages you might taste and see.

Others of you hear the name "Holy Spirit," and it makes you more suspicious than excited. Your guard shoots up. That's often because of unfamiliarity—you may have been shaped in a church tradition that more-or-less brushed over topics like the Spirit and his gifts. The supernatural events that pepper the pages of the New Testament were studied but never expected and certainly not pursued. And when that's been your experience, an introduction to a new expression of a familiar spirituality can feel threatening. Just as often, though, suspicion is born of familiarity—you may be recovering from a painful or manipulative spiritual experience under the banner of "Holy Spirit." And when you have been on the receiving end of a toxic charismatic environment, perhaps the safest place to stay is far away from anything that resembles your past. To the suspicious, I want to (re)introduce you to the Holy Spirit as a person to know and be known by, not a power to wield or an experience to force.

Finally, some of you are simply uninformed. Something like those sincere disciples Paul encountered in Ephesus: "'Did you receive the Holy Spirit when you believed?' They answered, 'No, we have not even heard that there is a Holy Spirit,'"[3] a statement aimed less at intellectual ignorance and more at experiential unfamiliarity with the full inheritance won for them in Christ. And that's probably the ideal starting place—a blank canvas on which to paint the expectation of an experiential spirituality. To the uninformed, the pages that follow are an invitation to wrap yourself in the biblical story until you find it has come off the page and into the daily grind of ordinary life.

The aim of this book is to offer readers from each of these three starting places a (re)introduction to the *person* of the Holy Spirit and an invitation to live, in the obligations and opportunities of ordinary life, clothed in the *power* of the Holy Spirit.

Part 1: When the Advocate Comes is rooted in the dialogue between Jesus and the disciples in John 14–17, tracing Jesus' words on that evening through holistic biblical metaphors that paint a picture of who the Spirit is and how we relate to God as Spirit.

Part 2: Spiritual Experience as Everything or Nothing offers an important explanation of two limited but tragically common ways of relating to the Holy Spirit that today's church tends to gravitate toward, illustrated through two lesser known New Testament characters. The aim of this section is to help readers identify how they've been formed or de-formed in relationship to the Holy Spirit, navigating what healthy growth in an experiential spirituality might look like from either end of the spectrum.

Part 3: Clothed with Power from on High is a thoughtful and practical consideration of some of the gifts and expressions of the Spirit's presence and power that are frequent on the pages of the New Testament but mysterious, abused, or absent in much of today's church. The aim of these chapters is to make the ministry of the Spirit accessible to ordinary people in search of an experiential spirituality.

In the end, my hope is that this book will bring the biblical story off the page and put language to your desire, converting desire into prayer and prayer into life—the Spirit-empowered kind of life here and now in a fallen world.

PART ONE

WHEN THE
ADVOCATE COMES

The Person of the Holy Spirit

But very truly I tell you, it is for your good that I am going away. Unless I go away, the Advocate will not come to you; but if I go, I will send him to you.

JESUS CHRIST (JOHN 16:7)

YOU AND I ARE LIVING through a historic cultural shift. In a single generation we've gone from the advent of the internet to the internet carried around in everyone's pocket. From social gatherings to social media. From hometowns where everybody knows your name to transiently bouncing from city to city with the freedom to reinvent yourself. From basic goods driving the economy to ideas and startups driving the economy. From a common, cultural spirituality to widespread suspicion of anything common when it comes to spirituality.

And whenever culture is changing, the church, which exists within culture and context, is changing with it.

Summarizing the message of Phyllis Tickle's book *The Great Emergence*, Presbyterian minister and author Marjorie Thompson writes, "We are undergoing the most recent of our every-500-year 'rummage sales'—an upheaval in culture and worldview that will inevitably reshape our faith interpretations and institutions as surely as the Great Schism of the eleventh century and the Great Reformation of the sixteenth Century."[1]

Thompson goes on to name the characteristics of this tsunami wave of change hitting the church: It is profoundly Spirit-centered, seeking discernment from deep listening. It is more concerned with right practice than with right belief. It is comfortable with questions and leery of answers. It embraces tension and paradox over the dualistic absolutes of right and wrong. It rejects hierarchical structure, welcoming shared leadership and democratic decision-making.

Today's young adults and the generation following them are far more open to experience than explanation. They're much more likely to try a yoga class or a mindfulness meditation app or even an hour in a Christian prayer room than listen to a sermon. And that's new.

Post—World War II generations wanted information and answers to hard questions, which is why books like *The Case for Christ* and *Evidence that Demands a Verdict* did so well. It was a heyday for apologists. *Win my mind, and you get my heart.*

But beginning with millennials, and increasingly in subsequent generations, a new era has dawned. Today's young adults are suspicious of experts, forever aware that there's always another perspective on any topic. But when a message we hear matches or resonates with our experience, that message wins our trust. *Win my heart, and you get my mind.*

This sheds light on the political toxicity in America and other Westernized nations. For example, whose view matters on immigration policy? Is it the politician with a Harvard background? Or is it the first-generation immigrant who fought countless personal battles to cross the border? Depends on who you ask.

The same holds true within the church. Whose opinion matters on suffering? Is it the pastor who studied the topic in a cozy office while sipping coffee and combing through commentaries? Or is it the person who's suffered, who's weathered the storm of an unthinkably difficult loss and made it through still clinging to Jesus? Most listen to experience before expertise these days, so when it comes to faith, what used to be "convince me" has now become "show me."

The doorway that stands open between the church and the broader culture is a thoughtful, experiential spirituality grounded in the person of the Holy Spirit. And yet within the church the very Holy Spirit Jesus was so eager to give us has become mysterious and divisive. We are desperate for a (re)introduction to the person of the Holy Spirit, who has become feared, forced, and—for the majority of us—simply a familiar stranger.

Part 1 of this book is a (re)introduction to the person of the Holy Spirit. Its aim is a rediscovery of all that was behind Jesus' baffling claim that God's indwelling presence through the Spirit was (and is) even better than his bodily presence with us. In recent times God's Word and God's Spirit have been unfortunately pitted against one another, with many churches magnifying one while neglecting the other. In Christian tradition, however, Word and Spirit are viewed as interconnected, complementary mediums working together to introduce us to the intimate mystery of God's person. In this first section I hope to reunite what has recently been tragically separated.

Each chapter will trace a different biblical metaphor for the identity of the Holy Spirit but follow the same path:

- **Creation** explores the Spirit's presence and role in Genesis, discovering the Spirit at the story's very beginning.
- **Roots** traces the Spirit's presence through the scenes of the Old Testament.
- **Jesus** represents the Spirit's active role in the incarnation, life, death, and resurrection of Christ.
- **Then** is a look at the way the New Testament church related to the Spirit.
- **Now** is an invitation to know and practice the Spirit's relational presence here and now.

ONE

THE FAMILIAR STRANGER

When the Advocate comes, whom I will send to you from the Father—the Spirit of truth who goes out from the Father—he will testify about me. And you also must testify, for you have been with me from the beginning.

JOHN 15:26–27

"YOU GUYS ARE GONNA LOVE CROQUET! It's just like mini golf, but you get to hit the ball harder with these big mallets."

I was trying to salvage an obviously disappointing scenario. As a father of young boys, I've become an expert at two critical skills: hyping an upcoming fun experience and redirecting disappointment. Some days, like this one, I attempt both back to back.

I was on the Isle of Wight, a charming English island just south of the mainland, and it was a perfect day in May. That morning we'd spotted a mini golf course, and my sons Hank and Simon (six and four years old at the time) had their hearts set on trying it out. They'd even planned the color of their golf balls and invented a scoring system they'd use to determine a champion.

They were elated as we wound our way up the quaint, narrow

roads toward the old, run-down amusement park. We had to park a good ways away, and after a long walk up a steep embankment, we finally crested the hill and laid our eyes on the object of their desire. Closed.

I couldn't believe it. It was 5:07 p.m. Apparently they had closed at 5:00 p.m. Employees were flooding out. Gates were being locked. There were hours of daylight left, but this place was a ghost town, even on a summer night fit for Ferris wheels and funnel cakes.

That's when my second skill set kicked into operation. I'd spotted a croquet set in our host's garden-side shed the day before. My boys had never heard of croquet, a game more fit for pleated pants and senior living facilities than rowdy little ones.

As we walked back down that steep hill toward the car, I took each of their hands in mine and began telling them how much better croquet in the yard was gonna be than what they'd been anticipating—a mini golf club in one hand and a dripping vanilla soft serve in the other. I gave it my best shot. They weren't buying it.

John's account of Jesus' final night reads a lot like that to me. Jesus said something hard to understand, even for the most seasoned disciples: "I'm going away, but that's going to make it so much better!"

John 14–17 records one long conversation between Jesus and the twelve disciples. Wedged right between the Last Supper and his arrest in Gethsemane, Jesus cracks a wry smile and says, "Look, my days with you are numbered. But I'm sending you my Spirit, and that's even better!" That's the sentiment, at least. Jesus' actual words were, "But very truly I tell you, it is for your good that I am going away. Unless I go away, the Advocate will not come to you; but if I go, I will send him to you."[1] So according to Jesus—and he's remarkably clear about this—the Holy Spirit is a staggering improvement to a direct, face-to-face conversation with God in the flesh. God's indwelling presence through the Holy Spirit surpasses God's bodily, human presence through Jesus. That's what he said.

The most interesting part of that, at least to me, is this: We don't buy it.

We're not alone. The twelve didn't buy it either. They were looking at Jesus the way Hank and Simon were looking at me on that downhill walk to the car on the Isle of Wight. They'd been planning and anticipating their imagined experience of Jesus' Kingdom—the size and location of their thrones, the respective legacies they'd leave behind—all of which, to be fair, were rooted in a common interpretation of the biblical prophets, not a narcissistic ego. The point is, they already had an ice cream–dripping, mini golf–playing vision in mind, so all this talk of Jesus' exit and the Holy Spirit's arrival sounded as appealing as croquet back in the yard.

The disciples didn't buy it, and neither do we. Honestly, how many of us would trade our current experience with the Holy Spirit for one face-to-face chat with Jesus? Basically all of us, right? Regardless of maturity, commitment, gifting, education, or tradition, most of the people dotting pews across the globe on any given Sunday are a bit underwhelmed with the experience of the very promise that got Jesus so excited. The "better plan" that made Jesus momentarily giddy on the march to his own execution? We'd trade it back if we could.

The biblical story presents a triune God—three persons, one God; a God in communion—Father, Son, and Spirit.

We generally get the Father. He's God in heaven parenting all of us, his children.

We know the Son. Jesus, who came and lived among us, sharing our human experience.

The Spirit, though, has become something of an urban legend. We've all heard the rumors, but has anyone actually spotted the yeti? The Spirit is like that person in your friend group who you've spent hours in a room with but never personally talked to. You've been associated with them by proxy, related to them primarily through association. Inevitably, some moment comes around—mutual friends all get up from the dinner table simultaneously, or the two of you arrive first, or you end up carpooling together or something—and there's that inevitable moment when you're stuck for a few minutes, just the two of you, trying to make conversation. And it's so awkward you're dying inside. That's the Holy Spirit for so many in today's church.

The 2014 "State of Theology" survey conducted by Ligonier Ministries, which aimed at uncovering commonly believed heresies in the modern church, asked participants this true-or-false statement: "The Holy Spirit is a force, not a person." Fifty-one percent of respondents said "true," 42 percent said "false," and 7 percent said "I don't know."[2] In contrast, the 2022 "State of Theology" survey showed that 60 percent of committed Christians answered "true."[3] Meaning nearly two-thirds of American Christians believe the Holy Spirit, the third *person* of the Trinity, is a force to be wielded, not a person to know and be known by. A familiar stranger.

ONE: CREATION

> In the beginning God created the heavens and the earth. Now the earth was formless and empty, darkness was over the surface of the deep, and the Spirit of God was hovering over the waters.[4]

The Holy Spirit is not a New Age, mystical teaching introduced after Jesus. The Spirit was present at creation, named in the Bible's opening lines. In Hebrew, the original language of Genesis, we read, "And the *ruakh* of God was hovering over the waters." The Hebrew *ruakh*, like its Greek counterpart *pneuma*, can be translated into English as either "spirit" or "breath."[5]

Later in Genesis we come to this passage: "Then the LORD God formed a man from the dust of the ground and breathed into his nostrils the breath of life, and the man became a living being."[6] Genesis often uses the phrase "the breath of life" to describe living creatures.[7] We only have life because God breathes life into us. Sometimes the phrase "breath of life" uses *ruakh* (the same Hebrew word used in Genesis 1:2 to talk about the Spirit of God) and sometimes it uses a roughly synonymous word. But the concept is clear: The same Spirit (or breath) of God that orders and fills all of creation in Genesis 1 fills people with his divine life—his Spirit. Hang on to that.

TWO: ROOTS

Throughout the Exodus story that follows on the heels of Genesis, God's presence is described as a dense cloud. A cloud guides the Israelites through the desert toward the promised land. A cloud visibly descends on Mount Sinai when God meets with Moses face-to-face. Eventually God instructs Moses to build a *tabernacle*, which is translated from a Hebrew word meaning "tent."

Sounds a bit ridiculous, right? Build God a tent so he can go camping with us?

It may sound ridiculous to the twenty-first-century Western reader, but in Moses' ancient Near Eastern world, this was a revolutionary thought. The ancients imagined deities bound by location, like a sun god and moon god, the god of the stars or of the sea. A tabernacle meant Yahweh was strikingly personal—God walking with his people, staying with his people, among his people in their sleeping and waking, coming and going, grieving and celebrating. This conception of a personal God was so strikingly unique that the prophet Isaiah borrowed the image of Moses' tent for his discussion on the reunification of heaven and earth.[8]

The final verses of the Exodus story include this description: "Then the cloud covered the tent of meeting, and the glory of the LORD filled the tabernacle."[9] The cloud—the visible presence of

God leading the people—took up residence among the people and moved in to dwell with them. Later the scene repeats itself in the commissioning of Solomon's temple—the glory of the Lord, in the form of a cloud, took up residence among God's people.[10]

While there is unthinkable beauty in a God who would come this close to make a home with his people, there is equally a disappointing wrinkle in each account. It's good because God's presence is clearly among his people, and that's wildly intimate. But it's incomplete because even with this God, there are still significant limits to the intimacy.

Moses could not enter the tabernacle he built when the cloud first filled it, because God's glory was inapproachably powerful. And as for the rest of the people? On one occasion when God was meeting with Moses on Mount Sinai, anyone who even set foot on the base of the mountain was to be put to death.[11]

The same goes for Solomon's temple. The priests couldn't even perform the worship service when God showed up. God's glory was so powerful that no one doubted his existence but neither could they stand in his presence. No one could experience real intimacy with the powerful God of the temple. In fact, only the high priest could enter the portion of the temple known as the holy of holies, where the presence of God dwelt, and only once a year on the Day of Atonement, or what is commonly referred to today as Yom Kippur. And even then, when the high priest went in, the other priests tied a rope to his ankle so they could retrieve his body in case he dropped dead before the glory.

God's presence with his people highlighted his fierce commitment to and pursuit of them, as well as the persistent distance between an "east of Eden" people and a holy God. The tabernacle and temple represent an era of presence without intimacy—good, but incomplete. This isn't to say that no one experienced intimacy with Yahweh, but to know and speak to God face-to-face (as we see with Abraham, Moses, and others) was exceptional, not common.

THREE: JESUS

The Gospel writer John opens his account by tying the person of Jesus to the ancient revelation of Yahweh. "The Word became flesh and made his dwelling among us. We have seen his glory, the glory of the one and only Son, who came from the Father, full of grace and truth."[12] The English "made his dwelling" is from the Greek *skenoo*, which literally translates "to set up a tabernacle." The most direct translation is, "The Word became flesh and *tabernacled* among us."

The Old Testament pattern was to build a tabernacle and God would fill it with his glory (his presence). John opened his gospel by describing Jesus as a tabernacle filled with God's glory (his presence). The glory of God that filled the tabernacle has now filled the body of Jesus. He is the living, breathing, walking, talking tabernacle.

The pages that follow reveal that this is much more than just a clever play on words. It's the basis for understanding Jesus' life. He went around acting like he *was* the tabernacle. One of the reasons Jesus got in so much trouble with the priests of his day was because he did a whole bunch of things you weren't supposed to do outside of the temple.

For instance, he walked around telling repentant people, "You're forgiven." And the priests balked at that notion. If someone needed grace, they went through cleansing rituals, offered the required sacrifice for the offense, and were granted forgiveness by the qualified priest *at the temple*. That's more than just legalistic ritual. They got it from Moses, the founder of the tabernacle. It's in the Torah, so who does this renegade rabbi think he is?

But here's Jesus, again and again—no cleansing, no temple, no sacrifice, no priest—"Do you want to repent? Okay. You're forgiven. Free." And he would make an even more provocative claim than the one just mentioned from his disciple John. Jesus said, "Destroy this temple, and I will raise it again in three days."[13]

Jesus said this while standing in the temple built by Herod, which was one of the architectural wonders of the ancient world. The Jews were offended and dismissive, mistaking the reference for the building itself. "But," John tells us, "the temple he had spoken of was his body."[14]

Jesus was talking about his human body, which, of course, was filled with the gift of God's life breath, harkening all the way back to Genesis. But he was also claiming that he was a tabernacle, the physical embodiment of God's divine life—the living, breathing, walking, talking temple.

And when Jesus referred to the presence and glory of God, he was talking about the Holy Spirit. His sentiment is, "You may be building a container for God's presence, but so am I. I am making *you* the container for God's presence just as I originally intended at creation. What I'll build in three days (through my death and resurrection) is the reality to which the temple was always meant to point."

FOUR: THEN

On resurrection evening, Jesus breathed on his disciples and said, "Receive the Holy Spirit. If you forgive anyone's sins, their sins are forgiven; if you do not forgive them, they are not forgiven."[15]

What could that possibly mean?

Well, remember how Jesus got in trouble for going around doing things tradition said you could do only in the temple? He promised his Spirit to his followers and commissioned them, "Now you do all those temple-specific things I've been doing."

Does that mean you and I go around forgiving sins? No, and yes. It means people should experience the forgiveness of God through God's people who carry his presence. Jesus commissioned his followers with the very presence and power that they'd seen in him, not as a comforting theory or a poetic metaphor but in actual practice.

Just as Jesus, filled with the Holy Spirit, acted as a living temple, so now he commissions his disciples to be filled with the Spirit and act in this world as living temples—indwelled with the presence of God.

The rest of the Bible is essentially a bunch of ordinary people "tabernacling." Ordinary people filled with the Holy Spirit and carrying the ministry of Jesus forward.

FIVE: NOW

The apostle Paul wrote to the Corinthian church, "Don't you know that you yourselves are God's temple and that God's Spirit dwells in your midst?"[16]

In ancient Greek there are several different words for "you," making clear when we're talking about a single, individual "you" or a communal "you." In English, we've got only the one "you," which, I imagine, is why the American South invented "y'all." It's also why, in this passage, we read the clumsy translation "you yourselves," because we're talking about the collective, not the individual—the communal "you."

To paraphrase Paul, "There's still a tabernacle. There's still a place in the world where God's glory dwells. It's y'all." It's the church, not the building or structure or governance but the collective lives of Jesus' followers. As a community, all who call Jesus "Lord" are bound together by the Holy Spirit.

There's even more, though. Paul continues to build on this train of thought: "Do you not know that your bodies are temples of the Holy Spirit, who is in you, whom you have received from God? You are not your own; you were bought at a price. Therefore honor God with your bodies."[17]

This time, it's the singular "you." You—your individual, physical body—is now the dwelling place of God through the Holy Spirit, which I think is just as he originally intended when he breathed his *ruakh* into the first humans in Genesis. Every follower of Jesus has been filled with the very Spirit that filled Jesus.

The Holy Spirit is the familiar stranger in the background of the Bible's every turn, inching closer and closer to us as the story moves forward. To gather the whole biblical theme up in a single sentence: God's Spirit has been given to *us* and to *you*.

WHOEVER

On the night of his arrest, Jesus said: "Very truly I tell you, *whoever* believes in me will do the works I have been doing, and they will do even greater things than these, because I am going to the Father."[18]

Jesus has made us all into tabernacles filled with the presence and power of God, doing the very things we've seen him doing. Who's it for? Whoever. The power of God has been shared with whoever will receive it. Eugene Peterson writes, "It is the lived conviction that everything, absolutely everything, in the scriptures is livable. Not just true, but livable . . . This is the supernatural core, a lived resurrection and Holy Spirit core, of the Christian life."[19]

The Holy Spirit makes the impractical practice-able. This is what the gifts of the Holy Spirit are all about: making the totally impractical (the supernatural, the miraculous, the gospel ministry of Jesus) not only possible (in extreme situations by super-spiritual people) but practice-able (by ordinary people tabernacled by an extraordinary God).

It must break the heart of Jesus that the very Spirit he was so eager to give has become unknown, feared, and divisive.

UNKNOWN

Many believers look at their lives with the honest, sober admission, "If this life, the one I'm experiencing right now, is everything the resurrection made possible, I'm underwhelmed." There is a troubling gap between biblical promise and the actual life of the modern disciple.

People flock in and out of churches, ordering their lives around the teachings of Jesus, building on the foundation of the Father's love, but totally unaware of how close this triune God has come, how entirely he has given himself to us.

Widely respected evangelist Billy Graham once said, "Everywhere I go, I find that God's people lack something. They are hungry for something. Their Christian experience is not all that they had expected, and they often have recurring defeat in their lives. Christians today are hungry for spiritual fulfillment. The desperate need of the nation today is that men and women who profess Jesus be filled with the Holy Spirit."[20] Billy Graham, who traveled the globe, seeing the church in every variety and form, concluded that the church is missing the Holy Spirit, longing for the Holy Spirit, needing the Holy Spirit.

FEARED

The Gospel writer Luke opens his sequel to the life of Christ with the summary phrase, "all that Jesus began to do and to teach."[21] The order of this statement is crucial—do, then teach. Jesus frequently gave people an experience of God first, then explained that experience second.

Some tend to be suspicious of experience and enamored with explanation. "Teach me everything first, and then maybe I'll be open to the experience."

It's worth remembering that the biblical story is made up of Holy Spirit–saturated historic accounts of ordinary people experiencing God in various ways, and then, on the other side of that experience, discovering roots for their experience in the unfolding revelation of Yahweh to and through his people.

In his book *More*, Oxford scholar Simon Ponsonby emphasizes experience as essential for real transformation: "I purposefully emphasize the word 'experience,' and will seek to show from the Scripture the importance of experience. A nonexperiential religion is suspect, for it fails to deal with the totality of our being."[22]

Many are led to experience by hunger and curiosity, but at least as many—maybe more—by honest, holy discontent. Clinical psychiatrist Curt Thompson writes, "Despite the interest in spirituality in much of the West, and North America in particular, our overall experience of God's power and life-giving vitality is often limited. We often see life in Jesus as being more about survival than about grace, adventure, and genuine, concrete, life-giving change."[23]

A life deeply rooted in Scripture is absolutely essential for a healthy relationship to God, self, others, and the world at large. Equally essential, though, is a life deeply rooted in the Holy Spirit, who leads by experience and functions in *partnership*, not competition, with the explanatory Holy Bible.

DIVISIVE

For several generations across the Western church landscape, there has been a noticeable divide between "Bible churches" and "Holy Spirit churches": Certain churches major on teaching the Bible thoughtfully, intellectually, and exegetically, but the experience of the Holy Spirit is largely absent. Other churches major on the ecstatic experiences attributed to the Holy Spirit but tend to diminish the Bible to a shallow script for spiritual pep talks.

The Holy Spirit, depicted by Jesus as the bonding agent to unify the church, has somehow become the dividing agent of the church. God, whose name is Jealous, must be so jealous for the unity of his Bride.[24]

The Kingdom of God is not an either/or kind of kingdom but a both/and kind of kingdom. The Bible *and* the Holy Spirit. Thinking *and* feeling. Teaching *and* experiencing. Contemplative *and* charismatic. Biblical exegesis *and* words of prophecy. Preaching the gospel *and* signs and wonders.

The church of Jesus Christ is a people who together emphatically declare, "Yes to the Holy Bible!" and in the same breath, "Yes to the Holy Spirit!" "Yes" to the intimate presence and supernatural power of a God who wants to be with us and even within us.

ARE YOU AVAILABLE?

If there's a band that defines my generation, it has to be Coldplay. I've honestly never been the biggest fan, but they've been releasing platinum albums and touring stadiums around the world for much of my life, coming of age alongside me and my peers.

On a Saturday night not too long ago, I climbed into bed with a few tears running down my cheeks because I'd just finished watching the Coldplay documentary, *A Head Full of Dreams.* I was brought to tears not by my own nostalgia or the band's story as a collective, but by the individual story of Will Champion, the band's drummer.

As it turns out, when the band was formed, Will didn't know how to play the drums. He was a musician but not a percussionist. His college roommate was a drummer and had an audition with the other three band members, who had already booked their first gig but needed someone to hold rhythm.

The guys turned up, but Will's roommate was a no-show. Yes, that's right. This poor sap no-showed for an audition for the band that would define a generation.

Because of the urgency of their upcoming concert date, and because Will was there in the dorm room explaining his buddy's unfortunate absence, the three band members asked, "Hey, would you just give it a shot? We've gotta rehearse these songs, and given that you're musical, maybe you could hold a simple rhythm?"

They rehearsed. Will sounded a lot like a guy who didn't know how to play the drums, but he held his own enough to join them for that first gig in a small English club. And the rest, as they say, is history.

Will Champion wasn't qualified. He wasn't skilled, practiced, or trained. He was available.

God has never cared much for the qualified, but he's shaped history through the available. This isn't about being qualified. It's not about being skilled, practiced, or trained. Are you available?

TWO

BREATH

All this I have spoken while still with you. But the Advocate, the Holy Spirit, whom the Father will send in my name, will teach you all things and will remind you of everything I have said to you. Peace I leave with you; my peace I give you. I do not give to you as the world gives. Do not let your hearts be troubled and do not be afraid.

JOHN 14:25–27

I WAS PLAYING MIDDLEMAN, trying to find a way to cut through the inevitable awkwardness of bringing together two separate groups of friends. One group consisted of a few close companions from my local community. The other group was made up of a few out-of-town visitors. I was the common denominator.

We'd gathered for prayer in the empty sanctuary of our church on a Saturday morning. As we prayed, Gavin, who'd only met John the previous evening, offered a picture he believed just might be from God: John was on a beach with an octopus all wrapped around him. He was trying to wrestle his way out of the tentacles

21

but couldn't get free. He was screaming for help as he tossed and turned on the shoreline.

It was all very *Jaws* meets sci-fi, and as Gavin tried to draw meaning from the image, he said he believed it had something to do with sleeplessness and wondered aloud if John was wrestling with anxiety or nightmares interrupting his sleep.

Immediately, tears shot down John's cheeks, his head dropped into his hands, and he began to tremble as he wept. Gemma, John's wife, knowingly wrapped her arms around him. Gavin's prayerful vision had accessed a real-life memory—a painful memory for John—deeply submerged under layers of trauma.

The biblical authors, introducing us to the person of the Holy Spirit through the metaphor of breath, reveal the pursuing nature of God's love—the way God's love is given not only to the head where it can be learned and understood but poured directly into our hearts where it can heal our deepest pains.

ONE: CREATION

As noted earlier, the Spirit was present at creation. "The Spirit of God was hovering over the waters" could equally be translated, "The breath of God was hovering over the waters." Or, with a little imagination, "God was breathing on the unformed chaos."

What happens when the breath of God meets unformed substance? Creation. God speaks creation into being—sun and moon, land and sea, vegetation and animal life. When God speaks, when his breath—his Spirit—goes out, creation happens. Further, when God created people something unique happened, unparalleled in any other aspect of creation. He put his breath into them.

Why would God give human beings his breath (his Spirit)? The first thing we learn about God on the opening page of Scripture is that he is creative. He gives his creative capacity to us when he gives us his Spirit. The first biblical command is "be fruitful and increase in number."[1] Create! Rule over creation. Work these raw materials into an ecosystem.

And despite the forbidden fruit fiasco, this theme of divine creation continues. God re-creates within a fallen and corrupted world in the same way he created out of nothing: by his breath, his Spirit.

TWO: ROOTS

God's creative work is not limited to Genesis. In fact, one could argue that the theme of God as Creator becomes more pronounced *after* the fall. As the biblical story moves from the ravages of the fall into the hope of redemption, God continues to speak through the prophets—and two Hebrew words appear frequently: *bara*, often translated as "create," and *ruakh*, which we've seen is often translated as "breath."

The verb "create" appears most frequently in Isaiah, not Genesis. Isaiah is a collection of prophecies from the devastating period of Israel's downfall leading to their exile.

The Jewish people were conquered by Babylon, and many were subsequently marched as prisoners of war across six hundred miles of desert and forced to live at the bottom rung of a foreign society in a foreign land. And it was there, in the incomprehensible sorrow of forced displacement, that the verb "create" appears most frequently in the Old Testament, culminating in the hopeful promise, "See, I will create new heavens and a new earth. The former things will not be remembered, nor will they come to mind. But be glad and rejoice forever in what I will create, for I will create Jerusalem to be a delight and its people a joy."[2] The Spirit of God who hovered over creation, bringing life and order from chaos, hovered over this new formless void—bringing life from the rubble of exile and the pain of loss.

Eugene Peterson writes, "'Create' is not confined to what the

Spirit did, it is what the Spirit does."[3] From horrific devastation emerges a hopeful promise: The Creator is the Re-Creator.

Ruakh also continues to show up as the story builds—a recurring promise to re-create the world by divine breath, just as God did at first. It's a theme in Job, the Psalms, Isaiah, and Zechariah, but perhaps most clearly in a vision of the prophet Ezekiel.

Ezekiel sees a valley filled with human bones—dry, lifeless, long-dead bones. And he's walking around among them. That's where God asks him a question:

> "Son of man, can these bones live?" . . .
>
> Then he said to me, "Prophesy to the breath; prophesy, son of man, and say to it, 'This is what the Sovereign Lord says: Come, breath, from the four winds and breathe into these slain, that they may live.'" So I prophesied as he commanded me, and breath entered them; they came to life and stood up on their feet—a vast army.[4]

There it is, again and again and again: *Ruakh*. Breath. Spirit. "Ezekiel, breathe into the old dry bones, and they'll come alive again." It's a promise! A reenactment of Genesis when God breathed into Adam's lungs. God says, through a picture, "I'm going to give my Spirit to my people again, just like I did at the beginning, before sin entered the picture."

The Creator who breathed life into dust to create people filled with his Spirit is also the Re-Creator who breathes life into the lifeless, refilling people with his Spirit.

THREE: JESUS

Jesus' ministry began not with his voice but the breath of the Creator. When Jesus was baptized by his cousin John in the Jordan, the voice of God spoke.

"And a voice from heaven said, 'This is my Son, whom I love; with him I am well pleased.'"[5] The creative power of God's breath, spoken over Jesus at his baptism, is clearly at work through Jesus during his entire ministry.

Following his baptism Jesus began teaching, and the response was telling. "The people were amazed at his teaching, because he taught them as one who had authority, not as the teachers of the law."[6] The English word "authority" is the Greek *exousia*, meaning "the power or ability to act." So when this Jewish audience noted that Jesus spoke with authority, they meant that his speech seemed linked to the action of God.

God's speech and God's action are inseparable; he says, "Let there be light,"[7] and instantly there's light. Jesus' speech had that same authority. As his ministry unfolds, God's action is inseparably linked with Jesus' voice. When Jesus forgives, people receive it. When he says stand up and walk, people lame from birth actually stand up and walk. When Jesus says, "Be opened," to the mouth of the mute, the ears of the deaf, or the eyes of the blind, they're opened. When Jesus says, "Come out of him, you evil spirit," even the supernatural forces of darkness obey him. And when he speaks to the bones of his dead friend Lazarus from the opening of a tomb, breath refills Lazarus's empty lungs and he walks out alive. The vision of Ezekiel becomes real in Jesus.

But what started in Jesus doesn't end with Jesus.

FOUR: THEN

In John 20, on the eve of his resurrection, Jesus appeared to his disciples. "He breathed on them and said, 'Receive the Holy Spirit.'"[8] He offered his breath for their lungs, his Spirit for their dry bones.

Interestingly, the word translated as "breathed" in this passage is the Greek word *emphysao*, which is extremely rare, appearing only here in the whole of the Bible. The Greek translation of the Old Testament, known as the Septuagint, includes this word a handful of times, though—including Ezekiel 37 and Genesis 2. From ancient days there has been an interpretive link joining God's breath filling his image bearers with life, Ezekiel's vision of re-creation, and Jesus' fulfillment of Ezekiel's promise.

What Jesus promised in John 20 was given in Acts 2. He told his disciples to go to Jerusalem and wait, and at the perfect time they'd receive the gift of the Holy Spirit.

> When the day of Pentecost came, they were all together in one place. Suddenly a sound like the blowing of a violent wind came from heaven and filled the whole house where they were sitting. They saw what seemed to be tongues of fire that separated and came to rest on each of them. All of them were filled with the Holy Spirit and began to speak in other tongues as the Spirit enabled them.[9]

As an isolated incident, this is beyond strange—floating, flaming tongues and supernatural foreign language translation? In the context of the broader story, though, it makes perfect sense. As Yahweh did "in the beginning," as Ezekiel saw in a vision, as Jesus taught with authority, so now ordinary people like you and me begin to speak words that create.

Those in the upper room open their mouths and the words spoken are heard in the ears of the crowd in their various native languages, the result of which is the creation of a brand-new kind of community—one the world had never seen. Various people groups, cultures, and languages together as one family. It's the rebirth of the world God created—the one he was too stubborn and too in love with to give up on.

Don't miss this. The story is coming together. In Genesis the world was born when the breath of the creative God filled the empty lungs of people, and they came alive to go on creating. In

Acts the world was reborn when the breath (Spirit) of the creative God refilled the empty lungs of people, and they came alive to go on creating.

That means Ezekiel's vision isn't an isolated incident for a special prophet at a special time. It's for everyone. *"All of them were filled with the Holy Spirit."*[10] The gift of the Spirit isn't for spiritual elites. It's for everybody!

Beginning on the day of Pentecost, God's Spirit was breathed into a growing community of people, quickening them with resurrection life and enabling them to cocreate in partnership with God. When this Spirit-filled group of individuals tells the gospel story, people's lives change, walls between people groups fall down, and a new community that defies every social structure is born within the Roman Empire. These ordinary people pray with the authority of Jesus and prison doors are opened, people are redeemed, and diseases are healed. They dream dreams, see visions, and speak words of knowledge that graft Ethiopian officials and Gentile landowners into the story. They offer a word of encouragement and the once insecure stand with remarkable courage.

And, of course, they also get it wrong. They continue to wrestle with sin. They go through highs and lows, supernatural miracles and ordinary conflicts, miraculous answered prayers and grief-inducing unanswered prayers. Because we're talking about the Spirit of the living God indwelling ordinary, imperfect people, both realities mingle together in individual lives and whole communities. Supernatural power in ordinary vessels: the most costly treasure in jars of clay.[11]

FIVE: NOW

So there I am, playing middleman between friend groups. Gavin is describing a prayerful picture of John struggling to wrestle himself free from an octopus on the beach—a picture he believed had something to do with bouts of anxiety in the night.

At this point in the story, there's something you need to know, something I wouldn't find out until later: John had been battling sleeplessness for months. Long hours and high pressure at work had his mind cranking anxiously, even in his bodily exhaustion. He was a designer at a boutique startup, and he was talented and successful enough that Google regularly tried to poach him. But the pace and culture of the workplace had him overworked, chronically anxious, and unable to sleep.

It started with anxiety that would wake him a couple hours into sleep. He'd regularly find himself unable to rest his racing mind and sitting up in the living room—frustrated and reading a novel to pass three or four hours while waiting for the sun to come up.

More recently, though, John had been having a recurring dream in which he felt paralyzed—like dark forces were pinning him down. He'd try to speak out but couldn't. He'd try to scream but no sound would emerge. Eventually he'd cry out a prayer in Jesus' name, commanding the darkness to be gone. And he'd wake up actually screaming that prayer aloud in bed, waking himself and Gemma.

The sleeplessness began in the first year after the birth of their daughter, Ember. After a grueling, decade-long battle with infertility, John and Gemma believed that Ember's arrival was a sure sign that a new season of joy and freedom was dawning over their family. But the two years since had turned out to be the opposite—an unexpected and tragic death in the family, a horrific turn in Gemma's health requiring intensive and time-consuming care, a battle with workplace anxiety for John. It all felt like one thing after another constricting him, like the tentacles of an octopus were wrapped around him, squeezing and suffocating.

When God put that odd image into Gavin's imagination, a relative stranger to John, he was doing it for the purpose of re-creation. God was reaching into John's past to uncover a traumatic experience that his love had not yet touched.

The mess that followed as John trembled and wept that Saturday morning was the power of the Holy Spirit re-creating in John from the inside out. The Spirit of God gently but certainly overpowered the grip this anxiety maintained on John's life.

It's one thing to be told God loves you, to memorize comforting Scripture verses, and to sing lyrics of redemptive promise. It's another thing entirely for that love to be targeted and channeled directly to your most personal wound, coating it like a healing balm. It's the same message, but the difference in delivery changes how we are able to receive it.

Among his final words to his disciples, when speaking about the Holy Spirit, Jesus said, "All this I have spoken while still with you. But the Advocate, the Holy Spirit, whom the Father will send in my name, will teach you all things and will remind you of everything I have said to you."[12] Later in the same conversation, Jesus added, "He will not speak on his own authority . . . he will take what is mine and declare it to you."[13]

According to Jesus, the Holy Spirit is a particular kind of teacher: one who helps you *remember*. To put it plainly, the Holy Spirit has no original content. The ministry of the Holy Spirit is entirely about translating the teachings and promises of Jesus in a way that forms us at the deepest level—rewriting our neural pathways and enabling us to embody our redemption. The Holy Spirit pushes the teachings of Jesus from the head, where they can be understood, down into the heart, where they can heal our emotions and become a new foundation for us to live from.

Jesus teaches that God is a prodigal Father running out to meet me, clothe me in royal robes, and welcome me to the home I wandered away from before I really knew what I was leaving. The Spirit makes this real to me. As high as the heavens are above the earth, that's how great God's love is for those who fear him.[14] The Spirit helps us experience that love. As far as the east is from the west, that's how far he has removed our transgressions from us.[15] The Spirit enables us to experience the reality of that forgiveness.

The apostle Paul adds, "God's love has been poured out into our hearts through the Holy Spirit."[16] Influential figures through-out church history, from Augustine to Anselm to medieval mystics, have understood the Holy Spirit as the personified love between the Father and the Son. The Holy Spirit, according to Jesus, is not a consolation after Jesus' bodily departure. Quite to the contrary, the Holy Spirit is an intensification of his presence and a deepen-ing of his love, even from what his closest followers experienced in knowing him face-to-face.

A. W. Tozer, in *The Knowledge of the Holy*, argues that we all know God "explicitly" and "implicitly." We all hold explicit beliefs about God, which we come to logically and can explain to others. But we also hold implicit beliefs, the relational patterns that live beneath our logic in our gut and define the way we relate to God. Our explicit knowledge is the way we know God intellectually. Our implicit knowledge is the way we know God relationally and experientially.

Likewise, the Hebrew word often translated as "know" or "knowledge" is *yada*. But this doesn't refer only to intellectual understanding. That's a very new, Western way to think about knowledge. In the Hebrew imagination, something wasn't known until it was understood relationally and experientially. *Yada* is a relational, experiential kind of knowledge. That's why in some translations of the Old Testament the word "know" is used as a euphemism for sex: "Now Adam knew Eve his wife, and she conceived."[17] Obviously this does not mean that Adam learned something new intellectually about Eve. This refers to the most intimate sort of relational, experiential knowing. The Holy Spirit was given that you may *know*—experientially and relationally—the true life of everything Jesus taught.

The deepest transformation begins with a redefining experience. We cannot think or will our way to reformation at the deepest level. We need outside intervention, some profound moment of clarity, a watershed moment, or a redefining experience to serve as a new foundation upon which to build.

Twelve-step recovery groups acknowledge this principle through the insistence on a higher power to which the person must appeal to experience freedom. The twelve steps, which are based on biblical principles, demand something more than gritted teeth. They require a clear plan and an accountable community for the deepest sort of reformation. All of those are essential components, but apart from a spiritual experience they are insufficient.

The Holy Spirit is the conduit of spiritual experience. Modern-day spirituality tends to err on either side of the spectrum. Some camps glorify experience as if that alone will suffice for holistic spiritual formation, which it cannot. Others champion repentance, intention, accountability, and information as the means of transformation, attempting to rebuild apart from the needed foundation of redefining spiritual experience. Jesus seems to be saying that the Holy Spirit is the conduit of both: the channel through which God's love is poured experientially and the great Counselor reminding us of Jesus' teaching that we may build upon that experiential foundation wisely.

But there's even more involved. The same Spirit empowering our own experience of God's love empowers us to live as conduits of the same love toward others. Brennan Manning beautifully wrote, "If I am not in touch with my own belovedness, then I cannot touch the sacredness of others."[18] The Spirit assures us of our belovedness, and that assurance then frees us to uncover the sacredness in others. The Spirit fills our ordinary lungs with *ruakh* so that we can join God in his re-creative work in his people and his world.

John's trembling tears of healing are an example of the Spirit's work. The inciting incident that led to this messy display of healing power was a thought in Gavin's imagination during an otherwise quite ordinary moment of prayer. Consider the fragility of this moment—how easily Gavin might have explained away the thought as a distraction to deflect instead of an invitation to investigate.

God has placed the treasure of his presence and power in ordinary clay vessels like you and me, and that means John's profound healing hung in the balance between Gavin's imagination and his lips. He had to take the risk of verbalizing a thought that turned out to be prophetic in order for John to experience God's love being poured into his heart.

When Gavin opened his mouth in that sanctuary, he surely knew he was opening himself up to well-intentioned awkwardness and potential embarrassment—or, just maybe, the co-creative, redemptive power of the living God. In all honesty, he didn't know which one. All he knew for sure was that the only way to find out was to lovingly, gently, kindly *risk*.

How often might you or I withhold redemptive power, forfeiting our blessed role as God's co-creative image bearers for the sake of saving face? How often are we held back by discomfort? How much redemption is hanging in the balance of my willingness to take God seriously enough to risk?

What started in Acts doesn't end there. The main character holding the plot together—the Holy Spirit—hasn't gone anywhere. The divine breath in the lungs of the early church is alive in us. If you are a follower of Jesus you have been filled with the Holy Spirit, who pours the teachings of Jesus directly into your heart and enlivens you with co-creative power for the sake of the world.

THREE

WATER

I have much more to say to you, more than you can now bear. But when he, the Spirit of truth, comes, he will guide you into all the truth. He will not speak on his own; he will speak only what he hears, and he will tell you what is yet to come. He will glorify me because it is from me that he will receive what he will make known to you. All that belongs to the Father is mine. That is why I said the Spirit will receive from me what he will make known to you.

JOHN 16:12–15

IT WAS A WET, GRAY SATURDAY IN JANUARY—the sort of winter day I've grown accustomed to in Portland. We were driving up to Mount Hood where, in less than an hour, the drizzle would turn into a magical snow globe, perfect for sledding. Hank and Simon, five and three years old at the time, had dozed off in the back seat. Felix sat next to me in the passenger's seat.

I met Felix while volunteering at an organization serving dinner to the houseless and hungry. He was in the rehabilitation program, nearing the end of his first year of sobriety. One thing led to another, and through serving side by side Felix and I grew into friends.

I'd swung by the sober house to pick him up and now, stuck in traffic on our way out of the city, Felix and I were talking the way you do on a road trip—meandering conversation about anything and everything, letting the dialogue wander.

"Tell me about your kids. I've never heard you talk about your kids," I said, filling a lull in the banter.

Felix is the father of two, both in their early twenties, a son and a daughter. He hadn't seen either of them in over a decade but had occasionally told me stories of when they were Hank and Simon's age—when he was still in their lives. That was before a string of prison sentences exceeding two decades, a bout with drug use, and a long absence that their relationship had never recovered from.

So I asked about them—their names, where they lived, what they were doing. And he just got quiet. Eventually I looked over, and he was softly weeping, this hulking giant of a man wiping tears from his weathered cheeks. He kept opening his mouth in an attempt to respond, but the emotion wouldn't allow him to get a word out.

Felix had served three separate prison sentences. He'd used and sold drugs. He had a thousand nights he couldn't remember. And then he met Jesus, and we'd celebrated God's forgiveness together! But this—the dad he wished he'd been and still couldn't forgive himself for not being—this was the untouchable place in him, the shame he kept covered, the one wound he'd convinced himself God's grace couldn't reach.

The New Testament is unflinchingly honest about both the power of God and the suffering of this world. The book of Acts tells plenty of stories of supernatural power, God's indwelling presence working in ordinary people in miraculous ways. But it's equally chock-full of suffering, confusion, and pain.

If you tell the story of the Holy Spirit apart from the world of suffering, you rip the story from its context and turn a gritty, real-life hope into a fairy tale—a hollow fable that's entertaining in peace but powerless in chaos. This creates a false division between the heart of God and the power of God, a misconception that God is more present in a dimly lit auditorium full of inspired people than in a car stuck in traffic on a road trip.

That won't do because the truth is that every last one of us is Felix in that passenger seat, a living mixture of redemption worth celebrating and persistent patterns of chaos. We have all been rescued by a God of perfect love, and the plotlines of our redemption stories are breathtaking. But we all have unfinished storylines where pain is more apparent than renewal and suffering is more profound than rescue.

When the biblical authors use the metaphor of water to introduce us to the person of the Holy Spirit, they draw together what we are ever-tempted to separate: unflinching honesty about the suffering of this world and unwavering hope in a Redeemer who gets his work done in the darkest places.

ONE: CREATION

The Holy Spirit is introduced in the very beginning, with the Bible's famous opening line: "In the beginning God created the heavens and the earth. Now the earth was formless and empty, darkness was over the surface of the deep, and the Spirit of God was hovering over the waters."[1]

In the ancient Near Eastern world that Genesis emerged from, "the waters" did not evoke the image of a peaceful stream on a summer morning. "The waters" were feared, symbolic of chaos.[2] As the Old Testament moves forward, the sea continues to serve as imagery for chaos and disorder.[3]

With that context in mind, we might read the Bible's opening line like this: "In the beginning the Holy Spirit is hovering, waiting, and when the Father gives the word, the Spirit touches the chaos . . . and suddenly there is order." Light divided from dark. Land separated from sea. But there's more than just organization. There's life! In the place where there was once only confusion, dysfunction, and disorder, now there's delight, wonder, joy, and hope.

The description of Eden includes "a river watering the garden."[4] God has channeled the chaos waters, ordering them into a spring that becomes a river that gives life to the garden and beyond. From the Bible's first scene, we gather that the Holy Spirit doesn't just get rid of disorder. The Spirit makes the very place of darkness and fear an oasis teeming with full, free life.

TWO: ROOTS

Of course, just a page into paradise, all that order and life is corrupted. Adam and Eve rebel against God and he casts them out of Eden. And that's why the world we live in has a lot more in common with chaos than peace. It's why—though there are moments of delight, wonder, and joy—confusion, dysfunction, and disorder continue to haunt us.

As the story rolls on, water, which once symbolized the fearful unknown, comes to symbolize the promise of God made known—the Holy Spirit. The Spirit of God is described through the imagery of water in the poetry of Psalms and Proverbs; the prophecies of Isaiah, Jeremiah, and Joel; and by the Gospel writer John.

But the promise comes alive most clearly in the prophet Ezekiel, who saw a vision of a river that originated in a trickle running down the temple. It grew from a trickle on the steps to a flowing river as he followed the current east: the direction Adam and Eve walked out of Eden after the fall. The direction representing our human condition and the devastating reach for control that resulted in chaos, not order and death, not life. A river flowing east means this vision is for you and me and everyone else who's ever lived in chaos.

> Then he led me back to the bank of the river. When I arrived there, I saw a great number of trees on each side of the river. He said to me, "This water flows toward the eastern region and goes down into the Arabah, where it enters the Dead Sea. When it empties into the sea, the salty water there becomes fresh. Swarms of living creatures will live wherever the river flows. There will be large numbers of fish, because this water flows there and makes the salt water fresh; so where the river flows everything will live. Fishermen will stand along the shore; from En Gedi to En Eglaim there will be places for spreading nets. The fish will be of many kinds—like the fish of the Mediterranean Sea. But the swamps and marshes will not become fresh; they will be left for salt. Fruit trees of all kinds will grow on both banks of the river. Their leaves will not wither, nor will their fruit fail. Every month they will bear fruit, because the water from the sanctuary flows to them. Their fruit will serve for food and their leaves for healing."[5]

The river flows east, bringing overwhelming life wherever it goes. Alongside the river, fishermen gather because fish of every kind are swimming in its current. Just as people of every nation, tribe, and tongue and of every socioeconomic bracket, every background, every degree of having it together and falling apart make up the family of God. Fruitful trees line the banks, yielding fruit that feeds the nations and leaves that heal diseases.

The river empties into the Dead Sea, known for its lifelessness. Because the waters are approximately 25 percent mineral, no fish or any other species can survive. But in Ezekiel's vision, when the river flowing from the temple spills into the Dead Sea, the waters are purified so that fish of every kind swim there. A once-lifeless place is now teeming with Kingdom life.

Into the very place of fear, confusion, darkness, and disorder, there's a promise: I'll pour out my Spirit, and it will be like an unstoppable current of life and peace.

Within Ezekiel's vision there's a twofold divine invitation.

The invitation to come. Before he even sees where the river is going, Ezekiel is invited into the waters, wading in deeper and deeper until he's swimming. That invitation was understood as an essential invitation to experience by the earliest Christians. The ancient Tertullian referred to Jesus as "The Heavenly Fish," and to Christians as "little fish."[6] The common Christian fish symbol, whose modern use has devolved almost exclusively into unbearable cheesiness, actually comes from a rich history of understanding the Christian life as swimming in the waters of the Spirit.

The invitation to become. To become a part of the current that heals the world. The Spirit-empowered lives of Jesus' followers spill into the hopeless, hurting, and helpless places in our world, resurrecting the dead and renewing life.

THREE: JESUS

In John's gospel, Jesus turns Ezekiel's future vision into a present invitation, but how he does so is, to be entirely honest, awesomely rebellious and a touch angsty.

The story starts, "On the last and greatest day of the festival . . ."[7] The festival where it all goes down is the Feast of Tabernacles or *Sukkot* in Hebrew. It was a weeklong festival where the entire nation of Israel traveled to Jerusalem and camped in tabernacles (tents).

In Brooklyn, where I lived and ministered for twelve years, my neighborhood was home to the largest Hassidic Jewish population anywhere in the world outside of Jerusalem. Walk through that neighborhood on the right week in autumn and every balcony, terrace, or patio on every apartment building will have a homemade shelter on it. Those families sleep on their patios in homemade tabernacles celebrating *Sukkot*.

During that festival, people slept in tents all over the city of Jerusalem and gathered daily for jovial worship at the temple. On the seventh and final day of *Sukkot*, "the last and greatest day of the festival," crowds gathered at the temple steps for the culminating ritual. Priests carried large cisterns of water from a nearby spring to the temple, and while the crowd sang the psalms, the priests poured water from the altar down the temple steps, creating a stream flowing out from the temple toward the east. It was a living reenactment of Ezekiel's vision, an embodied way for a whole nation to pray together and ask God to bring the promised river of living water.

This was a holy moment. It was *the moment* the whole festival had been building to, the high point of a religious high holiday. Crowds belting out the psalms till their throats were sore, priests turning a prophetic vision into a living picture for all to see, tears of longing glossing the eyes of old and young, and in that very moment, "Jesus stood and said in a loud voice, 'Let anyone who is thirsty come to *me* and drink. Whoever believes in *me*, as Scripture has said, rivers of living water will flow from within them.'"[8]

Jesus was making a dramatic interruption timed to extend a twofold divine invitation that would have been instantly recognizable for those familiar with the prophecies of Ezekiel.

The invitation to come. "Are you thirsty? Come to *me* and drink. *I am* the living river. What you're waiting on in the temple you can find in me."

The invitation to become. To become a part of the current that heals the world. "All who come to me, the source, will become the source. A river of living water that heals the world will flow from within you."

Everything the river exemplified in Ezekiel's vision, Jesus became in the world. He left paradise to come after us, who had wandered east. He called his disciples "fishers of people," like Ezekiel's fisherman on the banks.[9] He fed the hungry and healed the sick, like the trees lining the riverbanks. Through his death and resurrection, Jesus poured life into a place of death.

And for those who came to him, who took him up on the invitation, the promise came alive in them, too, but not right away. John adds an important line of narration to the scene: "By this, he meant the Spirit, whom those who believed in him were later to receive."[10] John notes that Jesus was referring to the Spirit when he blurted out that perfectly timed interruption, but he's quick to add that the promised Spirit was not given in that moment.

FOUR: THEN

The Spirit Jesus promised in John 7 is given in Acts 2, when the disciples are in Jerusalem for yet another religious festival, Pentecost. Like the previous festival, this one is remembered not for the temple ritual but for the divine interruption. Peter, like Jesus, stands to explain: "Exalted to the right hand of God, [Jesus] has received from the Father the promised Holy Spirit and has poured out what you now see and hear."[11]

The river of living water has been poured out. Ezekiel's vision has come to life in our midst. You won't find it in the temple. The river of living water is now streaming forth from the lives of all who come to drink, just as Jesus promised.

And as the story unfolds in the pages that follow, everything the river was in the vision, the church became in the world. They fed the hungry, healed the sick, and proclaimed the good news. They weren't a holy huddle in a sacred building. They were a river flowing east—overwhelming dead places with unstoppable life.

The thematic introduction to the Holy Spirit through the metaphor of water that began on the Bible's first page reaches a crescendo on the Bible's final page. "Then I saw 'a new heaven and a new earth,' for the first heaven and the first earth had passed away, and there was no longer any sea."[12]

The apostle John's vision of heaven is not a distant utopia in the sky but heaven and earth reunited as one. But what's with the "there was no longer any sea" bit? Seeing the sun set on the coastal horizon might be as close to heaven on earth as it gets. Why would God dry up the Pacific when his Kingdom comes in full? Unless, of course, this isn't promising the drying up of the ocean but the drying up of chaos—the end of suffering, pain, and disorder.

John's heavenly vision continues, "Then the angel showed me the river of the water of life, as clear as crystal, flowing from the throne of God and of the Lamb down the middle of the great street of the city. On each side of the river stood the tree of life, bearing twelve crops of fruit, yielding its fruit every month. And the leaves of the tree were for the healing of the nations."[13]

It's Ezekiel's river and Eden's river before that, the one that flows from the temple into the Dead Sea. It's Jesus' river, the Holy Spirit that flows from within you into the world around you. It's the eternal current, that flows forever in the Kingdom to come when heaven and earth are finally one.

FIVE: NOW

The Spirit issues to us the same two-part relational invitation that we saw in Ezekiel's prophecy and in Jesus' words at the festival.

The invitation to come. Ezekiel was not invited to observe the river but to swim in its waters, to become a part of it. Jesus offered the same invitation in his holy interruption—to come and drink that we might become the source of the river itself. The Spirit's life is not for observation but participation.

That being said, a humble and honest read of today's church must conclude that we study the history but we don't expect the experience. We've been swimming in the Dead Sea far too long, so our hope for life—the kind Ezekiel dreamed of, the kind Jesus promised, the kind rumored of in the church's first thirty years—has been filtered through years of big theory and underwhelming experience.

It's not that we don't believe God could do it. It's not even that we don't believe God wants to do it. It's that it takes an *experience* to awaken hope in those who have only ever swum in chaos.

So instead of storming this river like kids on the first hot day of summer, we do our best to manage the chaos of our lives on our own, constantly reorganizing our circumstances, forever convinced that we can plan and life-hack our way to peace. We're managing from the riverbank instead of wading in. But we haven't been invited to observe the river; we're invited to swim.

On the final night of his life, Jesus said, "All that belongs to the Father is mine. That is why I said the Spirit will receive from me what he will make known to you."[14] In other words, "Everything I'm saying to you now will go from idea to experience when you receive the Holy Spirit."

It seems to me that the Christian life without experience of and reliance on the Holy Spirit works just fine—until it suddenly doesn't. Without participation, "come and drink" is just a worldview. It's the best and fullest of philosophies, but it's still just a worldview.

That'll work most of the time. It'll get you by in life's uneventful stretches. But then you're stuck in traffic on the way to go sledding, the boys asleep in the back, and at an innocent question Felix's shame is exposed. The words won't come, but the tears will. What do you do about those themes in your own story in which despair has swallowed up hope, shame stands taller than grace, and chaos seems more profound than redemption?

What do you do with that ongoing battle with infertility? The crushing grief of losing a loved one to an illness or an accident? Where does healing come from then?

What about when they hand you the diploma, or the promotion, or a seat at the table, or that badge of status? What happens when you get that but lose yourself somewhere along the way?

Or when you stand in front of your friends and family and

make wedding vows, and now you're a few years in and he's changed and so have you? You're somehow missing each other, and you're miserable. Where does the healing come from when the "forever" kind of promises get broken?

What about when that abuse you'd buried so deep resurfaces, and you're paralyzed in adulthood by events from childhood?

What do you do when the people who shaped your faith let you down? Where do you take the pain of seeing the community that welcomed you to the family becoming the community that hurts you most deeply?

A worldview can get you by on the ordinary days, but it can't heal you when chaos floods. Only the one who spoke order into the primordial chaos at creation can speak order into your chaos. That chaos is real, but the Spirit can create order from it and even make it a place teeming with everlasting life.

The invitation to become. The Holy Spirit brings personal peace, but peace isn't available to spectators. It's the reward of participation. And that's just the start. The Spirit also makes you and me part of the current of peace flowing through our chaotic world.

Jesus said "rivers of living water will flow from within them."[15] The apostle Paul added, "Do you not know that your bodies are temples of the Holy Spirit, who is in you, whom you have received from God?"[16] You are the temple—the source of the river that flows into the dead places and overwhelms them with life. This same Spirit who speaks peace over your internal chaos also sends you out as a peacemaker into the city.

Henri Nouwen recounts an old fable from the Jewish Talmud of a rabbi approaching the prophet Elijah and asking, "When will the Messiah come?"

"Go ask him yourself," Elijah replies.

"Where is he?"

"Sitting at the gates of the city," says Elijah.

"How will I pick him out of the crowd?" asks the rabbi.

"He is sitting among the poor covered with wounds."

That's who God is: "the wounded healer."[17]

The scandal of Jesus wasn't his power. It was his wounds and his apparent ordinariness. He held together the supernatural, loving power of God and the mundane suffering of this world.

Likewise, the scandal of the early church wasn't their success; it was their wounds and their ordinariness. When the government investigated this new sect, they "realized that they were unschooled, ordinary men, [and] they were astonished."[18] The leaders of the early church weren't particularly intelligent, compelling, attractive, or qualified. But they were filled with the same Spirit that filled Jesus.

The scandal of the Holy Spirit isn't power. If there's a Creator to be known, power has to be part of the equation. The scandal is the power of God dwelling in and operating through wounded, ordinary people. It's not your gifting that makes you an excellent candidate to be a river of life flowing into the dead places; it's your wounds. It's not the gifting or qualifications of today's church that makes us excellent candidates to reshape history and rewrite the stories of our cities through love; it's our wounds and our ordinariness.

"Anyone God uses significantly is always deeply wounded," writes Brennan Manning. "We are, each and every one of us, insignificant people whom God has called and graced to use in a significant way. On the last day, Jesus will look us over not for medals, diplomas, or honors, but for scars."[19]

THE POWERFULLY HEALED BECOME POWERFUL HEALERS

Felix sat there, weeping and speechless in the passenger seat. His past mistakes loomed with a shadow where he kept his deepest wound hidden from everyone. Even God. Even himself.

Felix knows about chaos. He knows—personally and inti-mately—the agony of addiction, the exhausting search for today's fix, the dehumanizing robbery of true life in the name of a numb escape. All of it. But he also knows about the Spirit whose waters flow into dead places and bring life.

Felix has become like a father to my children, particularly my youngest. Amos runs to him every Sunday morning at church and won't leave his arms. Each time I see Felix—one hand raised in worship, the other cradling my two-year-old little boy—I become tearful thinking of that Saturday stuck in traffic. I see the Spirit slowly but profoundly healing Felix's deepest wounds, hovering over his personal chaos, exposing his shame not to condemn but to restore.

Felix also serves as the head chef of Night Strike, Portland's largest ministry serving the houseless, hungry, and addicted. He learned to cook in prison, where he was assigned kitchen duty, and now cooks for hundreds of self-imprisoned, wounded individuals every Thursday evening. Felix came to Jesus to drink of living water, and streams of living water now flow from within him. Because from his wounds, God is healing others.

And, of course, Felix is still waiting. He's waiting on the day he lives in the redeemed city. Waiting for the God who will swallow up all his deepest desires in God's consuming presence. Waiting on the chaos to subside once and for all. He's waiting. But in the meantime? Felix has planted himself in the place where his wounds bleed hope to those similarly wounded.

God's not in search of a remarkable few who have it figured out. There aren't any spells to master. By the Spirit, the powerfully healed become power healers.

By Jesus' wounds we are healed.[20] And by our wounds we join in the healing of the world. The Holy Spirit's healing presence means that the addicted can become a safe harbor for others to find freedom. The depressed can be filled with incomprehensible joy and then give it away. The insecure can become courageous, inviting people into the very life they previously hid. The quick-tempered can be flooded with self-control, so that their transformation heals those they've wronged. The chronically anxious can become a non-anxious presence in their high-strung workplace, pouring living water into the Dead Sea. It goes on and on in every variety imaginable. Our deepest wounds, healed and redeemed by the Holy Spirit, become the sources of living water flowing with teeming life into the broken places in our world.

FOUR

DOVE

Very truly I tell you, whoever believes in me will do the works
I have been doing, and they will do even greater things than
these, because I am going to the Father. And I will do whatever you ask in my name, so that the Father may be glorified
in the Son. You may ask me for anything in my name, and I
will do it.

JOHN 14:12–14

MY EYES STRUGGLED TO ADJUST to the sunlight as I threw
the front door open and stepped out onto the sidewalk, squinting
as I fumbled for my sunglasses. It was the first day of spring,
not necessarily on the calendar but according to Mother Nature.
After what seemed like unending gray and cold, the sun was
glowing on this April Saturday, a literal light at the end of the
long winter tunnel.

I could feel my phone buzzing in my pocket as I walked down
the sidewalk, en route to meet my family at the park. Anyone
who knows me can attest to the fact that I *never* answer my
phone. I'm marginally responsive to text. But the actual "phone"

feature on my device could be deleted, and it'd be weeks before I'd notice.

I took a look and saw the screen glowing with the name of a friend from Bible college who I'd not spoken to in years. We'd studied side by side to become pastors, gone our respective ways, and lost touch. Intrigued, I picked up.

Raul told me he was sitting at the foot of a hotel bed. He'd just paid a sex worker. He sat there, swimming in an ocean of shame, drowning in it—unable to find the surface to come up for air.

There on the foot of that hotel bed, he opened up about a pornography addiction he'd battled for decades. It had come and gone in waves, and so had his resolve to fight it. Accountability partners, internet filtering software, prayer—none of it worked; he was nowhere near freedom. Occasionally he'd have a good run. But it never lasted, and with the next failure he was swallowed up again in that tsunami of shame that he'd nearly drowned in so many times before.

Booze seemed to help with the shame more predictably than God, so Raul numbed out a lot. Not every night, and he'd never described himself as an alcoholic, but the warm escape into a bottle became his rest. His pattern with lust continued to intensify until one night, on a business trip for the ministry he now served, he paid for sex from a stranger for the first and only time.

When the haze of the whiskey wore off, he was stuck with who he was and how lost he'd become. So he called me from the foot of a hotel bed.

At the time I received this call from Raul, I was about two years into leading a church plant in Brooklyn. And as a pastor just barely in the second half of my twenties, I was doing my very best to impersonate an adult and hide my profound insecurity.

One Sunday, when the worship gathering ended, someone from the congregation approached me at the front and said, "Wow! Tyler, I don't know how long you've been curating that content, but that was one of the best sermons I've ever heard." I could physically feel myself stand up straighter, my pitiful source of identity easily inflated (and deflated) by the perception of another. I left the church that Sunday gliding. I felt amazing. As I rounded the corner, right there on the sidewalk, God stopped me in my tracks with a gentle whisper.

"Tyler, no one was impressed by the 'content Peter curated' for the Day of Pentecost. In fact, no one noticed Peter at all. They were too busy responding to me."

As my pace slowed a little bit and I processed the unexpected, gentle deflation of my puffed-up false self, the kind whisper of the Lord went on. "Tyler, great content, but there was no power."

Only a confrontation with your own powerlessness will drive you to the power of the Holy Spirit. That confrontation comes in many forms—a dramatic wrestle with sin that has you pinned to the mat alone in a hotel room, or the subtlety of an honest realization that the very best you've got to offer in your own strength is insufficient to produce any lasting change.

I've got personal experience with both—destructive behavioral patterns I don't want but feel powerless to stop and the futility of trying to renew the world through gritted teeth and really meaning it this time.

Jesus must've had more in mind than a lifelong struggle we can't overcome, right?

If God is so strong, why does shame seem so much stronger?

Surely Jesus must've had more in mind than "how long have you been curating that content?"

If the Kingdom of God is not a matter of talk but of power, then why does it seem like much of the time we're all talk?

I eventually got desperate enough, and that's when I finally got acquainted with the familiar stranger we call the Holy Spirit. And so did Raul. And we both learned that when it comes to our calling to minister to the world, anything we can truly offer must be born out of our desperate weakness and God's unending kindness.

EVEN GREATER THINGS

In John's account of Jesus' last night with his disciples, the gift of the Holy Spirit is the central plot point. Among Jesus' last words to the twelve is the startling claim, "Very truly I tell you, whoever believes in me will do the works I have been doing, and they will do even greater things than these, because I am going to the Father."[1]

Jesus claims that his departure is a form of power sharing, and that his followers will begin to live and act in his supernatural power when the Holy Spirit comes in his stead. And that is what the biblical metaphor of a dove is all about: the elusive promise of supernatural power through the Holy Spirit.

ONE: CREATION

At Jesus' baptism, Scripture says the Holy Spirit descended on him, embodied in the image of a dove. Why the bird reference? Is this an author's attempt to spice up the literature with a well-placed simile? Not likely. All four Gospels use the same phrase, "like a dove,"[2] to describe the Holy Spirit's appearance at Jesus' baptism. What are the odds they'd all independently choose identical imagery?

To understand the magnitude of the claim packed into those three words, you've gotta hear it like the ancient Jewish readers did, and that takes us all the way back to the beginning. "In the beginning God created the heavens and the earth. Now the earth was formless and empty, darkness was over the surface of the deep, and the Spirit of God was hovering over the waters."[3]

TWO: ROOTS

Hovering. That's what the Holy Spirit is doing in the biblical story's opening scene. That's how most modern English Bibles translate the original Hebrew, at least. The Hebrew word is *rachaph*, and it's both rarely used in Scripture and difficult to translate.

You'll find this word only three times in the whole of the Bible. The first occurrence is here in Genesis, but the next doesn't come until Deuteronomy 32, in the midst of Moses' celebratory song for God's exodus rescue. Moses describes God's care for his people "like an eagle that stirs up its nest and hovers over its young."[4] This was the common use of the word in ancient days, and Jewish scholars understood the "hovering" of the Spirit at creation to mean something like "flutter," referring to the beating of a bird's wings.[5]

THREE: JESUS

Bring that context back to Jesus' baptism. The Gospels' authors are connecting the dots, making it obvious to their ancient Jewish contemporaries. The same Spirit hovering over creation in the beginning has come to rest, permanently, on this man Jesus, at his baptism. God created the world when his Spirit spread wings over the waters of chaos *like a dove*. God recreated the world when his Spirit spread wings over the waters of Jesus' baptism *like a dove*.

Quickly following on the heels of his baptism, Jesus walked into the synagogue on the Sabbath, took the liberty of choosing the Scripture reading for the day, grabbed the scroll of Isaiah, and publicly read, "The Spirit of the Lord is on me, because he has anointed me to proclaim good news to the poor. He has sent me to proclaim freedom for the prisoners and recovery of sight for the blind, to set the oppressed free, to proclaim the year of the Lord's favor."[6]

This is either a mic drop or a record scratch, depending on the listener. The phrase "Anointed One" is a translation of the term "Messiah." Jesus has selected a reading that all believe points to the promised and anticipated Anointed One, who will fulfill God's promises and redeem his people. The Anointed One is who God's Spirit rests on—not for a particular time for a particular purpose, but permanently.

As he completed the reading, Jesus rolled the scroll back up, handed it to the attendant, and began his first public teaching in his first public appearance since his baptism with, "Today this scripture is fulfilled in your hearing."[7]

Jesus just claimed to be the Messiah—the one permanently anointed by the Spirit of God.

The scandal that day at the synagogue may have been Jesus' messianic claim, but the big surprise to the modern reader, a couple centuries removed, isn't that Jesus claimed to be the Son of God. That rumor is in pretty wide circulation these days. It's the *way* Jesus did all the stuff that followed—the miraculous life that backed that messianic claim.

Jesus was baptized and the Spirit descended on him "like a dove" in Luke chapter 3. And in the verses that follow, Luke won't let up on the Spirit's essential role in Jesus' ministry:

- "Jesus, *full of the Holy Spirit*, left the Jordan and was led *by the Spirit* into the wilderness, where for forty days he was tempted."
- "Jesus returned to Galilee *in the power of the Spirit*."
- "Jesus stood up to read, and the scroll of the prophet Isaiah was handed to him. Unrolling it, he found the place where it is written: '*The Spirit of the Lord is on me*.'"[8]

By reading Isaiah 61 that day in the synagogue, Jesus claimed not only his identity as the Messiah but also that his power came from the anointing of the Holy Spirit.

We need to slow our roll a bit on this part because it addresses the central biblical question regarding the power of the Holy Spirit: How did Jesus do what he did? How did a human being walk around the earth working miracle after miracle? Where did his power come from?

There are two main ways of understanding how Jesus accomplished his many miracles.

By his own divine power

The idea that Jesus' ability to perform miracles came from his own divine power is probably the assumption many of us carry. It's been a common way of understanding Jesus for the past three hundred years or so. But three hundred years is relatively recent in the span of church history, so what are the origins of that idea?

Before the Enlightenment, the average person had a world-view that was infused with the spiritual. "The sun came up. God has made another day!" The scientific revolution and the Enlightenment ushered in the possibility of a much less spiritual worldview. "Well, actually, the sun 'rises' because the earth is spinning on an axis at about one thousand miles per hour and revolves around the sun at sixty-seven thousand miles per hour. You're a speck on a ball of matter flying through space. That's why the sun 'rises.'"

Along with these changes came new ways of imagining the "natural" and the "supernatural," with natural now referring to the realm "governed by the laws of science" and supernatural referring to that which "transcended the laws of science"—which in turn introduced a seeming rift between faith and science. As science's explanatory power exploded, faith and the supernatural were increasingly pushed to the margins. Perhaps it's no surprise that, alongside this shift, belief in the biblical God began to decline and Deism, "the divine watchmaker theory," emerged as a popular middle ground between Christianity and atheism.

And with Deism, new sentiments began to emerge about the relationship between Creator and creation. The argument went something like, "Even if there is a god who created the world, I don't believe he's intimately involved in human life. That god has moved on to other projects and left this world to run by natural, scientific laws."

H. S. Reimarus, writing at the height of the Enlightenment in the eighteenth century, proposed that Jesus was merely a human political reformer rather than the Messiah and Savior proclaimed by traditional Christianity. He initiated the quest for "the historical Jesus" behind the Jesus revealed in Scripture. Scottish philosopher David Hume and others rejected the miraculous entirely, and the same entirely naturalistic interpretation of the biblical story was adopted by Hobbes, Rousseau, and Voltaire, all of whom were highly culturally influential.

It was around this time that outspoken Deist Thomas Jefferson famously cut out all the miracle stories from the Bible, keeping the principles for morality and wisdom but stripping the story of all personality and power, a reduction known today as The Jefferson Bible. Collectively, these thinkers and others like them popularized a tolerance for a distant, uninvolved God to whom one may say prayers and offer respects but who is not intimately involved in the everyday—a God whose Kingdom may be in a faraway cloudy place but certainly not "on earth as it is in heaven."[9]

A response, equally new, began to emerge from the Christian church: "Wait, you can't remove the miraculous from Scripture. The miracle stories are *proof* that Jesus is God." So in the late eighteenth century, a new idea blossomed in popularity: Jesus was able to do what he did because he was the Son of God.

There is some truth in that. I don't believe that understanding should be thrown out altogether, but there are a number of problems with that idea. Most notably, all sorts of people do miracles in the Bible, not just Jesus:

- Back in the Old Testament Moses was the conduit for the ten plagues, the parting of the Red Sea, and bringing forth drinkable spring water from a rock. But he never claimed to be the Messiah.

- Elijah controlled the weather patterns, called fire out of the sky, and supernaturally raised a deceased child. But he never claimed to be the Messiah.
- Elisha blinded an entire army and later restored their sight, cleansed the skin of a leper, and also raised the dead. But he never claimed to be the Messiah.

And the list goes on.

- After Jesus, in the New Testament, Peter healed a crippled beggar, raised a woman from the dead, and—alongside the other apostles—performed many wonders and signs.[10]
- Paul brought a dead person back to life and was known so broadly for healing that he began sending handkerchiefs to the sick and suffering who he couldn't get to in person.[11]

There are plenty more examples, but the point is this: The Bible records all sorts of people doing all sorts of supernatural acts in ancient Judah and Israel and in the early church. But not a single one of them claimed to be the Messiah.

The belief that Jesus did miracles as proof of his identity is not the historic view of the Christian church and certainly not the view of the earliest Christian communities. It's a reactionary position born out of a defense against Deism, and it's only been around for about three hundred years.

The claim of Luke and the other Gospel writers is that the miracles of Jesus were signs of the in-breaking Kingdom of God. The long-awaited Kingdom had arrived, and it was being ushered in by the King, the Anointed One—Jesus.

Well then, how *did* Jesus do what he did?

By the power of the Holy Spirit

The historic belief of the church and the clear biblical evidence is that the supernatural power of Jesus came through the

Holy Spirit. Before his baptism, where the Holy Spirit descended on him "like a dove," Jesus lived thirty years, and as far as we know he didn't utter a word of teaching, work a miracle, or recruit a disciple. After his baptism, Jesus was constantly teaching, working miracles, and calling disciples. His baptism was the inciting incident that started it all.

Peter remembered it this way: "You know what has happened throughout the province of Judea, beginning in Galilee after the baptism that John preached—how God *anointed Jesus of Nazareth with the Holy Spirit and power*, and how he went around doing good and healing."[12]

This understanding of the Holy Spirit as the empowering agent of Jesus' ministry is so essential, because what started with Jesus didn't stop with Jesus. Scripture plainly states that the same Spirit that anointed Jesus anoints all who receive Jesus as Lord and Savior.

FOUR: THEN

Luke opens the book of Acts with the line, "In my former book, Theophilus, I wrote about all that Jesus *began* to do and to teach."[13] The implication, of course, being that this book is about what Jesus continued to do and teach. Only this book isn't about the life of Jesus. It's about the lives of his followers continuing all that he started.

And in the second chapter of Acts, in an upper room in Jerusalem where the disciples had gathered to wait according to Jesus' instructions, the Spirit descended and rested on each of them. Said another way, they were anointed at Pentecost by the very Spirit that anointed Jesus at his baptism.

Eugene Peterson connects the dots:

God gave us the miracle of congregation the same way he gave us the miracle of Jesus, by the Descent of the Dove. The

Holy Spirit descended into the womb of Mary in the Galilean village of Nazareth. Thirty or so years later the same Holy Spirit descended into the collective spiritual womb of men and women, which included Mary, who had been followers of Jesus. . . . The first conception gave us Jesus; the second conception gave us church.[14]

The remainder of the book of Acts is essentially the record of ordinary people, filled with the Spirit of Jesus, doing the stuff Jesus did. Acts covers the first thirty years of church history, and it looks eerily similar to the ministry of Jesus.

- Peter and John lead a prayer meeting that rattles the temple foundations.
- Philip teleports to an evangelistic encounter with an Ethiopian eunuch.
- Paul casts a demon out of an exploited, trafficked young girl.
- They speak words of knowledge that they could not know apart from God.
- They break down ethnic and socioeconomic barriers.
- And they serve food daily to the neediest in society.

To summarize, it's good news for the poor, freedom for the oppressed, sight for the blind, healing for the sick, and salvation for the lost—the continuation of the Spirit-empowered ministry of Jesus.

In fact, the supernatural ministry of Jesus became so common among the early church communities that Luke seems to have gotten tired of recording the specifics, turning instead to summary statements:

- "Everyone was filled with awe at the *many wonders and signs* performed by the apostles."

- "*With great power* the apostles continued to testify to the resurrection of the Lord Jesus. And God's grace was *so powerfully at work* in them all that there were no needy persons among them."
- "The apostles performed *many signs and wonders* among the people."[15]

Oxford scholar Michael Green summarizes, "The great characteristic of the New Testament Church is that it consisted of men and women who had received a living experience of the Spirit in their own lives. That is what turned the first disciples from a company of disappointed folk whose leader had died, risen, and left them, into a Church—reception of the Spirit."[16]

The very priests who opposed Jesus and colluded in his death reacted this way to his followers after Pentecost: "When they saw the courage of Peter and John and realized that they were unschooled, ordinary men, they were astonished and they took note that these men had been with Jesus."[17] The temple priests saw the church and thought, *Whatever was in Jesus is in them too.* Ordinary people filled with the Spirit of Jesus doing the stuff of Jesus.

And because God has seen fit to entrust extraordinary power to ordinary, imperfect people, there have been and will be abuses and misuses of the indwelling power of God. You, dear reader, might even be an innocent victim of such an abuse. And if that's your story, I'm genuinely so, so sorry. One biblical word for "power" is the Greek term *dunamis*, from which we get the English "dynamite." Dynamite can be used for good or bad, for building up or for tearing down.

To entrust extraordinary power to ordinary people is a risk. God takes empowerment risks on us, entrusting his name to a bunch of fumbling messes with egos and mixed motives. Sometimes we have experiences where we wish God would've just played it safe, would've kept his powerful Spirit all to himself. But we must remember that love is behind his empowerment. He risks on us out of love for us. In the words of Quaker activist and educator Parker Palmer, "Here is one of the great acts of love, empowering another person, knowing full well that person will probably make serious mistakes with that power, knowing that those mistakes may be costly even to the one who does the empowering."[18]

FIVE: NOW

Jesus, looking ahead to the gift of the Spirit, claimed, "Very truly I tell you, whoever believes in me will do the works I have been doing, and they will do even greater things than these, because I am going to the Father."[19]

There is significant debate among scholars about exactly what Jesus meant by "even greater things." Was Jesus referring to quantity or quality? Was he saying that because so many people will be filled with his Spirit, there will be a greater *quantity* of Kingdom works? Or was he saying that the people filled with his Spirit will carry his ministry forward and even further, making it not the ceiling but the floor for my life and yours? There's no way to know for sure. All we know is that Jesus definitely didn't mean "lesser and not as great works." And to fixate on the quantity versus quality debate is to miss the real heart of his point. Jesus is plainly telling us that "*whoever* believes in me will do my very works by my very Spirit."

The apostle John later summarized, "But you have an anointing from the Holy One."[20] Every follower of Jesus has been anointed with the very Spirit that anointed Jesus at his baptism and empowered his ministry. The divine dove has descended on every one of Jesus' followers.

Oxford theologian Simon Ponsonby pointedly asked, "If we have what the first Christians had, why do we not do what they did? We must conclude that either God gave them more than He has given us, or we have failed to avail ourselves of what He has given us."[21]

The early church congregations, where supernatural ministry was common, were made up of mostly illiterate peasants filled with the power of God. They didn't have theology degrees or biblical commentaries to consult. They didn't know their Enneagram numbers or Myers Briggs types. They had no clear strategies for church growth, conferences with renowned speakers, or even a completed copy of the New Testament. But they were desperate for the power of God. Desperate enough to risk, so they became practitioners.

And what they did, we study.

The early church was not a matter of talk but of power. The modern church is lots of talk, little power. American pastor and author A. W. Tozer diagnosed it when he said, "We have substituted theological ideas for an arresting encounter."[22] Wesleyan minister Samuel Chadwick made a similar observation: "A ministry that is college trained but not Spirit filled works no miracles."[23]

In his brilliant, vulnerably honest book *The Second Mountain*, *New York Times* columnist David Brooks writes of how he grew up loving film. As a sophomore in college, he went to one particular theater to see an old classic almost every night of the week. He then got his break into journalism by writing as a film critic. He'd sit in the screening room, notebook in hand, thinking he had his dream job, but something happened to him there: He stopped watching movies and started analyzing them. The notebook somehow became a wall between him and the story. By evaluating film, in his own words, "I lost the ability to have an authentic response."[24]

We don't get jaded into spectating because we *want* to sit back and evaluate. It happens in reaction to something real—an experience, usually a painful, disillusioning one. But in search of a more pure, authentic experience in the wake of that disillusionment, we often wall ourselves off from experience altogether. In an effort to become less naive, we accidentally become less human.

We become something like Brooks in a theater with a notebook open in his lap: critics who've lost the ability to have an authentic response.

Beware of mistaking sophistication (a good thing) for cynicism, bitterness, a lack of compassion, or minimizing the whole self to a brain on a stick (all detrimental things).

RING, ROBE, AND SANDALS

A son made off with his inheritance while his dad was still alive. He threw it all away on a gap year too wild to remember and ended up so hungry he shared a plate with the livestock at a farm where he bottomed out. Eventually, reaching the end of his rope, this son decides to make his way home, rehearsing his apology every step of the way. But his father ran out to meet him and forgave him before he could get a word out. The father even threw a party to celebrate, and everyone joined in (except the older brother, who was trying to earn love he already had).

God is like that father—that good and that forgiving. That's what life with God is like, an unearned homecoming celebration that never ends.

Charles Dickens called Jesus' story, commonly known as "The Prodigal Son," the greatest story ever told. In every retelling of that famous tale, including my own, we tend to leave a part out that Jesus emphatically included: the gifts—a ring, a robe, and a pair of sandals. The father gave his wayward son gifts symbolizing the authority the son carried as an heir to the whole estate.

So many of us are like the prodigal son without the gifts—lost sons and daughters who have returned home to find the Father running out to meet us. Beautiful! But we've tucked the gifts away in the closet. No ring. No robe. No sandals.

We are forgiven sons and daughters! But we're not remembering that we're heirs. We don't know how to live as heirs with authority over the Kingdom we've been entrusted with. The most subtle threat in the church today is that we'd live on the land of our Father, enjoying unmerited forgiveness, but never open the closet to clothe ourselves with his power. Forgiveness without authority.

You're home. You're forgiven. You're clean. You're renewed. You're free. It really is that good.

But there's even more.

There's power, authority, and miracles. There's grace not only to you but through you. There's faith, salvation, justice, hope, healing, and a Kingdom that crashes into this world when and where you least expect it.

Throw open the closet! There are gifts from your Father for you, just your size, handpicked only for you—a ring and a robe and sandals for your feet.

PART TWO

SPIRITUAL EXPERIENCE AS EVERYTHING OR NOTHING

The Church . . . can be in the way of God, but it never will cease to be also the way to God.

HENRI NOUWEN

IS THIS REALLY WHAT JESUS HAD IN MIND *when he said,* "Receive the Holy Spirit"? I didn't say it out loud, but that's the question I asked myself from the back of the uncomfortably humid high school gymnasium while otherwise ordinary-looking, middle-aged adults screamed and wailed, danced and fell prostrate. I was sweating. Maybe because of the heat. Maybe because of how awkward I felt, like a wallflower at a high school dance. A friend had invited me to attend this Pentecostal church plant with him. It was the opening worship song. I was already plotting my exit.

I didn't grow up in a charismatic tradition. For every amazing story of the supernatural, there's a sobering counter story of suffering, and for every curious reader of this book in search of a more experiential spirituality, there's a guarded reader in search of healing from a manipulative charismatic environment.

If we are to explore healthy and helpful models for knowing the Spirit as a person and living in the Spirit's presence and power, a good place to start is with humbly acknowledging that the church, both historically and in the present, tends to gravitate toward two unhelpful models: the expression of the Spirit's gifts as *everything* and the expression of the Spirit's gifts as *nothing*.

On one side of the aisle ecstatic expression is the main event, the most sought-after experience of the gathered church. Ironically, in these settings the third person of the Trinity is often minimized into a power source to tap into or a high to reach.

On the other side are those who are entirely passive when it comes to the Spirit's gifts and expressions. Despite professing openness to spiritual experience, they may see it as suspect or even dangerous.

These two unhelpful models are not new but ancient. In fact, Scripture gives two narratives that can teach us to recognize and resist these models: I call the stories "The Curious Case of Simon the Sorcerer" and "The Subtle Tragedy of Nicodemus." Acknowledging how we may have been malformed or deformed by unhealthy expressions of our spirituality is an important first step toward being formed by a healthy expression of our relationship with the Spirit.

FIVE

THE CURIOUS CASE OF SIMON THE SORCERER

When Simon saw that the Spirit was given at the laying on of the apostles' hands, he offered them money and said, "Give me also this ability so that everyone on whom I lay my hands may receive the Holy Spirit."

ACTS 8:18–19

NO ONE ELSE WAS IN THE ELEVATOR with Ben and me. Still, neither of us spoke as we were pulled upward, the floors of a Manhattan skyscraper clicking by early on a Thursday evening. I wasn't sure what to expect, and I knew that Ben wasn't either.

A couple months earlier, Ben's wife had pointed out that she'd never seen him cry. As far back as she could remember—through friendship, dating, and now several years of marriage—never once had she seen him shed a tear.

"Come to think of it," he later told me, "the last time I remember crying was more than twenty years ago."

Ben got angry sometimes—more than he cared to admit. But

there seemed to be an emotional block when it came to expressing sadness, disappointment, or grief—a block so significant that he decided it was worth exploring.

He asked me, his pastor and friend, for a referral to a therapist and subsequently requested that I attend his first appointment with him. So there we were, stepping out of the elevator and into the waiting room together.

I sat there praying silently and listening as the therapist asked Ben questions. This went on for more than an hour, until finally one of the therapist's questions accessed a certain memory.

When Ben was eleven or twelve he stumbled across pornography for the first time while on the family computer in the living room. He didn't go on a deep dive, but he did linger a bit. And at that moment his father, who was a strict disciplinarian and somewhat emotionally withdrawn, walked into the room and barked out, "Ben! What are you doing?" Ben, who had no idea someone was behind him, was terribly startled.

At this point in the therapy session, my friend began to wail. Not just a few stray tears. Sobs. He physically fell from his chair and onto his knees on the floor. Cries poured out of him as he struggled to speak—the weeping of a man who'd closed off this part of his emotions for decades.

In the days and weeks that followed, Ben discovered that his whole life—emotional availability, major directional decisions, his way of relating to others, even his view of self—was a response to the shame that, in that moment, had plunged into his gut and taken up residence. It was a wound that had never healed, so it told a story—a story that had come to define him.

PAIN THAT TELLS A STORY

Ben began to name and deal with his trauma. "Trauma" is a seventeenth-century word of Greek origin that literally means "wound." *Merriam-Webster* defines it as "a disordered psychic or behavioral state resulting from severe mental or emotional stress or physical injury."[1] Author and therapist Resmaa Menakem defined trauma as "a wordless story our body tells itself about what is safe and what is a threat."[2] Putting the three concepts together, author and pastor Rich Villodas defines trauma as "the state of woundedness and the story that comes from living in that state."[3] Trauma is not just being wounded. It's the story that arises from living wounded.

And that is, unfortunately, a troublingly common story when it comes to the ministry of the Holy Spirit in the local church. So many believers today have suffered painful moments when they felt manipulated or coerced by a spiritual leader, community, or environment, and that wound hasn't healed. It becomes a part of them. A traumatic experience based on a misrepresentation of the Holy Spirit tells a story in which the wound inflicted by another person becomes more defining than the promises of Jesus. A version of Christian spirituality then results that sidelines the presence and power of the Spirit altogether.

Like Ben, the believer living in the unhealed pain of such a traumatic experience tends to wall off parts of their spirituality, becoming "emotionally unavailable" toward God as a coping mechanism to guard against future pain. On the pages of Scripture we are offered both a diagnosis of such pain as well as a prescription for healing.

SIMON THE SORCERER

The first revival after Pentecost popped off in Samaria of all places. Philip couldn't miss. His teachings were bearing incredible fruit and accompanied by a demonstration of power that had jaws on the floor and people on their knees in surrender to Jesus.[4]

Notable among those riding the wave was Simon the Sorcerer,

a well-known spiritual figure in his own right, though he seems to have been playing with some variety of dark magic. Like the Egyptian magicians of Exodus, Simon was able to produce a supernatural manifestation in partnership with a spiritual force other than (and weaker than) Yahweh. But, just as with the magicians, Simon recognized direct access to the one, true God at work in and through Philip. In a turn of events that must have amazed the budding Samaritan church, Simon was among those who responded to Jesus and joined the early church community.

While there remains some debate about the sincerity of Simon's response, it is worth noting that Scripture initially presents him as a humble and sincere disciple of Jesus. To be baptized is an act of extreme humility, not necessarily an upward-mobility notch on one's spiritual belt—and it certainly wasn't a way to gain social prestige. Following this humble public spectacle, Simon followed after Philip, seemingly becoming his disciple and imitating his faith.

It's important we acknowledge the reality and sincerity of Simon's early days in the faith lest we dismiss him as a magician with whom only those reading tarot cards and playing with Ouija boards have anything in common. If you are a follower of Jesus who knows the surge of new life felt on the other side of surrender and salvation, you likely have more in common with Simon than you're tempted to think.

Eventually, news traveled about the awakening in Samaria, and Peter and John (the de facto leaders of the early church at this point) went to check it out, throwing gasoline on the proverbial fire.

Here lies the critical turning point in Simon's story. He has been amazed by Philip, and in Peter and John he notices a pattern—the manifestations of the Spirit are associated with the laying on of hands. He offers to compensate the apostles if they'll teach him to cast the same spell.

Simon is a sorcerer. He is well acquainted with spiritual formulas producing predictable results. He mistakes the Holy Spirit for a depersonalized power source like those lesser spiritual forces of his sorcery, grossly misunderstanding and distorting the gift given in the person of the Holy Spirit.

This time Simon does not respond personally and humbly as he did at first, and he is more concerned with becoming a respected practitioner wielding God's power than remaining a humble child receiving God's love. Simon wants technique, not surrender. He's after a method, not a Savior and Lord. He wants the gifts far more than the Giver.

The telling phrase from the account of Simon the Sorcerer comes near the beginning of the passage, a shadow that hangs over even his sincere beginning: "He boasted that he was someone great."[5] This is the seed that grows to distort all fruitful ministry. When the leader's ego is driving the pursuit of supernatural ministry, it distorts the Spirit's power from a creative force producing freedom to a controlling force producing captivity.

CONTROL

For decades American psychology was dominated by a single idea based on the discoveries of famed Harvard professor B. F. Skinner. He discovered that you can control an animal by directing its attention. Skinner tested this hypothesis on various species, producing the same result each time.

For example, he put a pigeon in a cage and waited until it was hungry. Then he added a bird feeder to the cage that released seed at the push of a button. If Skinner waited for a particular movement of the pigeon—like a jerk of the head in a particular direction, a jump to a certain stand within the cage, or a flap of the left wing—and released a few bits of seed at that precise moment, the pigeon would pick up on the pattern. Perform this routine long enough, and the pigeon will constantly, obsessively perform this trigger behavior, even if it stopped receiving the reward.

Skinner hypothesized that the same principle that held true

with pigeons, rats, rabbits, and pigs applied to human behavior as well. In other words, human beings are not free but driven by the obsessive compulsions of desire and gratification. Journalist Johann Hari summarizes Skinner's research: "Human beings, he believed, have no minds—not in the sense that you are a person with free will making your own choices. You can be reprogrammed in any way that a clever designer wants."[6]

To a degree, Skinner is right. Dr. Jeffrey Schwartz, a researcher on neuroplasticity and its relationship to OCD, defines the mind as "directed attention," and makes the case that an individual can literally rewire his or her brain through intentional directed attention.[7]

In some very real sense, we all are shaped by what we pay attention to. Fill your mind with violence, and you'll become more violent. Fill your mind with pornography, and you'll become more lustful and objectifying. Fill your mind with cynicism, and you'll narrow your eyes in suspicion and skepticism. And what holds true for negative thoughts and behaviors is equally true for positive thoughts and behaviors. Like poet Mary Oliver said, "Attention is the beginning of devotion."[8]

The trouble with Simon the Sorcerer is that he wanted the power of the Spirit as a means to an end. He wanted to use the Spirit's power to control situations, circumstances, and maybe even other people. That's the B. F. Skinner model for the life of the Spirit, and it doesn't work. "Where the Spirit of the Lord is, there is freedom."[9]

When we try to use the Spirit for our own ends, motivated by our individual egos, we seek to control others, contradicting the very Being whose power we attempt to call upon.

CREATIVITY

Mihaly Csikszentmihalyi was one of the few psychologists unimpressed by Skinner's work. He thought it was a depressing view of humanity, limiting the human person in ways that seemed undignifying.

While Skinner's work centered on utilitarian survival behaviors like food, Mihaly decided to devote his psychological study to a human behavior nearly as ancient and primal but neither utilitarian nor necessary for survival—the creation of art. He persuaded a group of Chicago painters to allow him to study their behavior for months. One aspect of their common creative process struck him: the way time seemed to evaporate as they painted. Often beginning in the morning, the artist would become so engrossed in her work that she'd forget even to eat, startled to look up to discover that it was dark out. The entire day had gone by in what felt, to her, like an instant. Time evaporated in the flow of creative concentration.

A second insight struck Mihaly. Despite the intensity of this devotion during the creative process, after a painting was complete the artist would set it aside and begin the next project. The ego, so central to Skinner's view of the human being as a desire-obsessed self-gratifier, seemed to have no hold on the creator. The artists did not gaze triumphantly at their work, invite others to behold what they'd done, or spend any time basking in the glow of their accomplishment. "When they finished," Mihaly said to an interviewer, "the object, the outcome was not important."[10]

The artist was not driven by measuring the greatness of the finished product but by the creative act itself. In his book *Flow*, Mihaly explores this principle beyond just painters, noting parallel human creative behaviors and contradicting Skinner's bleak "reward-based" view of human behavior. Flow, as Mihaly calls it, is a free state of creativity, a joyful and selfless human expression, a fly in the ointment of Skinner's bleak diagnosis.[11]

Simon the Sorcerer wanted the Spirit's power, but it was to gratify a self-centered desire for spiritual thrills and crowd-approval. It was to control, for the sake of his own ego, the very people God wanted to set free, for the sake of their own souls.

God is the original creator. He made human beings his image-bearers, commissioning us to co-create with him—an authority usurped and distorted by the serpent in the garden, an authority redeemed and restored by Jesus in another garden. The Holy Spirit is the divine creative force graciously restoring our place as God's image-bearing co-creators.

Creativity, which is a true and fitting expression of the Spirit's power, will always carry within it the two distinctive characteristics Mihaly noted in those Chicago painters. Those living in the Spirit's power will operate in flow, a free state of timeless creative focus, and they will be unattached to the fruit of their creative labor, driven instead by the act of co-creating in partnership with God.

Simon lacked these defining characteristics, leading to his rebuke.

SPIRITUAL THRILL-SEEKERS

Is this me? Am I Simon—seeking a spiritual thrill rather than the God behind the thrill and longing to wield power but trying to do so through formulas and methods when humility and hunger is the only way? Is the aim of my pursuit of the Holy Spirit to replicate a supernatural experience or live a more radically formed life?

In the modern church some people have been shaped in the tradition of Simon and champion good things like a hunger for spiritual experience and a wide-eyed belief in a supernatural life here and now. But at times these same people may err on the side of emotionalism and manipulation, leading to toxic environments built on hype and dramatization, where the experience itself is worshiped more than the God the experience is supposed to point to.

For those emerging wounded from this sort of background, searching for an authentic relationship with the Spirit will require trusting God rather than walling off parts of yourself from him or boxing God into "safer" confines. Those defensive measures, which are common responses to trauma, may protect you from the toxicity of your past, but they will also prevent you from authentic experience in your future. Trusting God as healer and guide allows the present Spirit, rather than past pain, to be the author of our stories.

IN THE NAME OF JESUS

Simon's story is more than a cautionary tale, though. It is held up as a contrast against that of another infrequently referenced but key biblical figure—Philip. While the overlap is chronological and literal, it also seems like Luke has constructed the narrative to juxtapose the two—Simon, a cautionary tale, and Philip, a model to follow.

Jesus promised power to guide his church, so the pursuit of the Spirit's power is good and necessary for every disciple. But all spiritual power comes only in Jesus' name, meaning that the power of Jesus must be channeled through the character of Jesus. Philip is commendable in his miraculous ministry and Simon detestable in his for one simple reason: Philip carried the *power* of Jesus in harmony with the *way* of Jesus; Simon did not.

Jesus' ministry was one of others-centered love, not ego infla-tion, costly sacrifice not platform building. For Jesus, living and ministering in the power of the Spirit included public miracles, but his private life was even more supernatural than his public life. Simon pursued the Holy Spirit with public spectacle in mind. Philip certainly inherited some public spectacle along the way, but like his rabbi, his hidden life was the supernatural core. All that happened in public was simply the overflow of what happened in secret.

If we are to carry the power of God incarnate, we must carry it in the way of God incarnate. Pursue the supernatural. Go after it with hunger and resilience and hope. Just be sure your feet are traveling on the narrow way of Jesus.

SIX

THE SUBTLE TRAGEDY
OF NICODEMUS

"You are Israel's teacher," said Jesus, "and do you not understand these things? Very truly I tell you, we speak of what we know, and we testify to what we have seen, but still you people do not accept our testimony. I have spoken to you of earthly things and you do not believe; how then will you believe if I speak of heavenly things?"

JOHN 3:10–12

THERE'S A WELL-KNOWN TALE, likely apocryphal, of Saint Augustine walking along the seaside. He always did this on Sunday afternoons between church worship gatherings. It rested his mind to walk and watch the waves wash in.

On this particular day he saw a young boy on the shore digging a hole and running with bucket after bucket of saltwater, pouring it into this hole he'd dug in the sand.

After watching a while, Augustine approached the boy and asked, "What are you doing?"

"I'm going to take that big ocean and put it in this little hole," replied the child.

The older man said kindly, "My son, that ocean is too big to place in that little hole."

The boy looked up at him and said, "Easier for me to take that big ocean and put it in this little hole than for you to take the big Trinitarian God and put it in your little mind, Bishop Augustine!"

And with that, the child disappeared, as he was actually an angel sent to remind Augustine just what he was trying to touch with all of his teachings.

That story has been passed through church history because it expresses a truth worth remembering. The dose of humility offered in the form of a boy with a water bucket is as important for us today as it was for Augustine, and I imagine it's like the truth dowsed on the Pharisee named Nicodemus in his midnight conversation with Jesus.

While Nicodemus's most substantial biblical appearance occurs in John 3, he makes three distinct appearances in John's gospel. To take in the full scope of his subtly tragic character development we must view his life through all three scenes.

SCENE 1: PULLING AN ALL-NIGHTER

Nicodemus was a member of the Pharisees, and not just any old member; he was the crème de la crème, a member of the Sanhedrin, the ruling council, and thus a respected overseer of ancient Israel's religious leaders.

The Pharisees, justifiably, tend to get a bad rap. However, John presents Nicodemus to us not as some corrupt power-seeker but as an academic elite whose heart had remained pure—humble

enough to keep his eyes open, looking for God, and asking questions. But all that he'd gained, all that he'd become, also meant
he had so much to lose.

Nicodemus introduced himself to Jesus with a leading statement,
implying a question without asking it outright. His comment was
aimed at Jesus' potential status as the long-awaited Savior: "Rabbi,
we know that you are a teacher who has come from God. For no one
could perform the signs you are doing if God were not with him."[1]

Jesus likewise responded indirectly, not answering Nicodemus's
implied question but rather the deeper question that had driven
Nicodemus to search out Jesus in the first place. "Jesus replied,
'Very truly I tell you, no one can see the kingdom of God unless
they are born again.'"[2]

Nicodemus had seen something in Jesus, who was actually
living the doctrines Nicodemus taught. He was curious about the
life beyond the theory. And he wondered if Jesus could show him
the way. "[Nicodemus] wasn't looking for theological information
but for a way *in*," writes Eugene Peterson, "Not for anything more
about the Kingdom of God but for a personal guide/friend to show
him the door and lead him in: 'How do I enter . . . ?'"[3]

Jesus' use of rebirth as a metaphor for entrance into the
Spirit-filled life carried particular significance in the first-century.
Non-Jewish converts to Judaism were called "children newly born"
in ancient rabbinic literature.[4] Jesus was speaking Nicodemus's
language here. He took a term reserved for Gentiles entering the
ranks of the chosen people as beginners, infants in the faith, and
applied it to a respected Pharisee, a member of the Sanhedrin.
"Here's how you enter the Spirit life: become like a newborn infant,
like a humble Gentile grafted in, like the lowliest member of God's
people, becoming least among those who know you as greatest."

Nicodemus wore the robes of a respected rabbi—garments
of status and prestige. He'd become somebody and developed an
identity of honor, safety, and comfort. The robes he wore meant
he had made something of himself—something good.

Jesus is cutting to the chase: "You've built an identity of your own making and done quite well. You've climbed the ladder, earned respect, established yourself. And after all that, your heart's burning for more. Here's the pathway to more: Humble yourself to the lowest place. Take off those heavy robes you've grown so comfortable wearing."

Nicodemus was living in the days the ancient voices foretold. It was all happening here and now, all around him. But to get in on it? Well, that required becoming like a child again, looking like and even feeling like a fool for a time, taking off the identity he'd made for himself.

"'How can this be?' Nicodemus asked."[5]

Maybe this reads to you like he's confused, that Nicodemus is taking Jesus' allegorical speech literally. "I can't get back inside Mom's womb." But some scholars suggest that Nicodemus wasn't confused. Instead, he may have been skeptical about the spiritual rebirth Jesus was describing—or he was willfully misunderstanding Jesus. While there's debate about Nicodemus's thoughts and motives in this conversation, I believe that Nicodemus felt exposed, so he retreated inside his robes, inside his training, back to his intellect and the identity he'd made for himself. He came for an explanation and Jesus gave it to him, but the path to enter the Kingdom would cost him.

You can see the Kingdom, speak about the Kingdom, even teach about the Kingdom, but if you want in—if you want the life of the Kingdom by the indwelling power of the Holy Spirit, then at some point you've gotta take the terrifying risk of experience.

SCENE 2: A VIEW FROM THE RIVERBANK

"On the last and greatest day of the festival, Jesus stood and said in a loud voice, 'Let anyone who is thirsty come to me and drink.

Whoever believes in me, as Scripture has said, rivers of living water will flow from within them.' By this he meant the Spirit, whom those who believed in him were later to receive."[6]

We've been here, remember? The Spirit as water.

We know Nicodemus was there for Jesus' show-stealing interruption. In fact, because Nicodemus was a Pharisee, he likely had a front-row seat or was even an active participant in the ritual of pouring the cistern down the temple steps when Jesus interrupted, "If anyone is thirsty . . ."

That holy intrusion was an act offensive enough to call for an emergency meeting of the ruling council. Amid the banter about what to do with Jesus, one defender raised his voice. "Nicodemus, who had gone to Jesus earlier and who was one of their own number, asked, 'Does our law condemn a man without first hearing him to find out what he has been doing?'"[7]

Nicodemus speaks up, outing himself as someone who's intrigued by Jesus, who still finds himself wondering, "Could he be the one the prophets talked about? Could he really be the source of the living river we're praying for?"

Having witnessed the power of Jesus, everyone's asking about the identity of Jesus. It's worth noting that the cadence with which people encounter Jesus in Scripture is typically experience, then explanation. We frequently see people reeling after a heartrending revelation of God's presence, then asking, "Who is this Jesus?" An unexpected spiritual experience sends the recipient in search of an explanation.

In some circles today, there exists a tendency to reverse the order: demanding the full explanation up front and *then*, once we've intellectually grasped the equation, experience is deemed safe. For many Christ-followers in post-Enlightenment Western culture, our temptation is to believe in Jesus' truth claims and even engage his practices but never experience his saving power and presence by the Holy Spirit.

God created every aspect of us, and he makes his appeal to

every aspect of us—our intellect, our emotions, our bodies, and our experiences. If we try to figure every last thing out before opening ourselves to experience, we are a child at the beach trying to get the ocean into a hole in the sand, and we'll never enter into the life of the Spirit.

I think Nicodemus, like many of us, wanted all his questions answered apart from the vulnerability of experience. If we want to know this King and live in his Kingdom, it can't happen from a safe distance. It can't happen by spectating. And it can't happen without risk and surrender.

Was Nicodemus standing front and center for Jesus' interruption on temple steps? Did his heart leap? Did he want to respond to Jesus' invitation? But "coming to Jesus that he might drink" would've meant taking off his robe. It would've meant leaving his self-made identity and becoming like a child again. It's one thing to come to Jesus at midnight with no witnesses. It's quite another to fall at Jesus' feet in the light of day on the very steps of the temple.

SCENE 3: A PROPER BURIAL

After Jesus' death on the cross, "Joseph of Arimathea asked Pilate for the body of Jesus. Now Joseph was a disciple of Jesus, but secretly because he feared the Jewish leaders. With Pilate's permission, he came and took the body away. He was accompanied by Nicodemus, the man who earlier had visited Jesus at night. Nicodemus brought a mixture of myrrh and aloes, about seventy-five pounds. Taking Jesus' body, the two of them wrapped it, with the spices, in strips of linen. This was in accordance with Jewish burial customs."[8]

There he is again. Nicodemus can't bring himself to come all the way in, but he can't stay away either. He's on the periphery, in the background of scene after scene, even helping give Jesus— crucified as a criminal—a proper burial.

At the very moment Jesus' disciples scatter because the cost of associating with him has never been higher, Nicodemus publicly comes closer than ever, causing some to speculate that he finally became a disciple of Jesus at this moment. Having beheld the beauty of God in his power—to heal, forgive, free, dignify, and save—did Nicodemus finally tear off his robes at the beauty of God willingly suffering in the name of love?

Some think so. But while John is careful to call Joseph a disciple in this passage, he never applies that term to Nicodemus. And we never read of Nicodemus in the other three Gospels, in Acts, or in any of the New Testament letters. There's no way to know for sure.[9]

What we do know for sure is that, at least on the pages of Scripture, Nicodemus remained forever at the fringes, a spectator rather than a participant.

FINDING MIDDLE C

Michelle Obama memorably recalls her first childhood piano recital in her autobiography, *Becoming*. She'd learned to play on her teacher's old piano with "its conveniently chipped middle C." Michelle prepared studiously and showed up ready to wow her family members with her honed craft.

At the recital, though, when she sat at the piano bench in front of the gathered crowd, she laid her fingers on the keys, and something was wrong. She couldn't find middle C. Not knowing where to start, she panicked. There was a period of complete silence—what felt like an unbearably slow full minute at least—as everyone waited for her to begin. Michelle was just frozen, running her fingers across the unfamiliar keys and trying to get her bearings. Then her teacher appeared at her side and "gently laid one finger on middle C." Michelle began to play, and as she found the right keys she lost herself in the music.[10]

What if living in the indwelling presence and supernatural power of the Holy Spirit requires that I feel like I'm regressing before progressing—like a child at her first piano recital who panics for a minute while trying to find middle C? And what if, from that place of naked vulnerability, I can get lost in the music again and find that I'm right at home?

To experience the life of the Kingdom, some of us who are comfortable in a version of spirituality that's filled with eloquence, honor, and predictability will have to get acquainted with a spirituality characterized by risk, humility, and power that's beyond our control. That's not easy, but I believe that if you choose vulnerability first, the melody will carry you. A man must become like a child again. Helpless and dependent, yes. But wild, joyful, and free too.

Theologians and writers have adopted Paul Ricoeur's concept of a second naïveté: when the very doctrine you know like the back of your hand widens your eyes and ravishes your heart again.[11] Like an old couple falling in love all over again, fifty years into marriage.

The subtle tragedy of Nicodemus is that in scene after scene, Jesus was awakening something in his heart. Nicodemus felt the breath of the Spirit on his own face. He stood on the banks of the Spirit's river and saw the life. Again and again he was drawn to Jesus, the one the Spirit rested on. But it seems that he couldn't let go of his robes so he could know true life.

The very life Nicodemus memorized on paper, sang about in psalms, and taught about in synagogues was on offer right in front of him. But he kept his robes on, held himself together, clung to his respectable self.

There is a common version of following Jesus that stays on the riverbank—delighting in his claims, marveling at what others experienced, enjoying the view, but neglecting to become like a child. The tragedy may be subtle, but it's a tragedy nonetheless when an admirer of Jesus fails to experience the full life of the Spirit.

FUNCTIONAL CESSATIONISM

In the Western church some believers have been shaped in the tradition of Nicodemus, which prizes good things like a high view of God's Word and the intellectual side of our faith but errs on the side of control or passivity when it comes to experience. For those emerging from this sort of background with a hunger for the Spirit, Christ's invitation to more of the life of the Kingdom will likely sound much like it sounded to Nicodemus. Become like a child again. Humble yourself. Risk feeling foolish. Risk the comfortable identity you've built for yourself. Maybe, with a little imagination, you can hear Jesus saying, "I want to give it all to you, holding nothing back, but you're gonna have to take off those robes you've grown so comfortable wearing."

Some Christians hold a cessationist position, meaning that they believe that the types of expressions of the Spirit's power and presence found on the pages of Scripture are no longer available to the church today. The general attitude among these individuals and communities tends to be suspicion of the unfamiliar. Rather than greet the invitation to experiential spirituality with enthusiasm, an attitude of distrustful skepticism toward any novel experience of God tends to hold sway.

Of course, there are always those who commit abuse and manipulation in the name of the Spirit. But that shouldn't cause us to adopt a skeptical attitude toward something that might deepen our experience of God. Ironically, it is frequently those thumping the Bible hardest who ignore the direct and straightforward biblical command to "eagerly desire gifts of the Spirit."[12]

When it comes to the ministry of the Holy Spirit, others manage to take only a baby step, landing on a passivity that I call functional cessationism. A functional cessationist often embodies some form of passive availability, saying, "If God wants to speak to me, I'm right here. If God wants to heal me, I'm open. If God wants to fill my mouth with a miraculous word of knowledge, fill my imagination with a prophetic image, or fill my hands with healing power, he knows where to find me." But they neglect to seek out the gifts of the Spirit and fail to develop a set of habits and mindsets that can foster openness and availability to the presence, power, and gifting of the Spirit.

This passive stance toward the supernatural ministry of the Spirit is a tactic never employed in other aspects of spiritual growth. Christians of every theological persuasion readily agree that a pursuit of God is necessary for spiritual maturity. A stance of passivity may avoid the worst of spiritual abuses, but it does so while subtly stunting spiritual growth and vitality.

Is this me? Am I Nicodemus? It may be worth asking, "When was the last time I prayed for miraculous healing? When was the last time a word of prophecy was shared with me or by me? When was the last time I had to seek out an explanation because my experience with God was a step ahead of my understanding of God?"

Am I Nicodemus? And if so, what are the robes I need to risk taking off that I might experience the gift of God's Spirit?

In his classic *War and Peace*, Leo Tolstoy introduces a character on military leave, home from the war. He spends every night at the local pub, wowing growing throngs of listeners for hours with stories of heartbreaks and heroics from his days on the battlefield. He could hold a room till last call with tales of war.

The only problem was that he'd never seen combat, never even left the safety of the barracks. Every one of his stories was true—the true stories of comrades returning from battle to rest in the evening. He'd heard these stories many times and then told and retold them again to the point where he lost track of the truth. He actually believed he'd lived stories he'd only heard.

We are in danger of this sort of life with God. We study and discuss the lives of the biblical saints and tell and retell their stories until we're convinced we've lived them, though all we've really done is heard the rumor of combat from the safety of the barracks.

Nicodemus was being invited to the front lines by the commander himself. But what a risk combat is when you've made a name for yourself as a storyteller and never set foot on the battlefield. May this not be the fate you and I accept. May we tune our hearts and ears to the voice of God calling us to step into the risk and joy of life with the Spirit.

PART THREE

CLOTHED WITH POWER FROM ON HIGH

A Life Empowered by the Holy Spirit

I am going to send you what my Father has promised; but stay in the city until you have been clothed with power from on high.

LUKE 24:49

"JUST SO I'M UNDERSTANDING YOU RIGHT, you want me to pray that God would miraculously heal your eyesight, like Jesus does in the Gospels?"

I asked this question to Irene, an older Malaysian woman who'd approached me at the front of the church following the worship gathering. Irene was experiencing a sudden and debilitating vision problem in her left eye, and she'd just received a diagnosis. Her eye required immediate surgery—a surgery for which she, a recent immigrant to the United States, had neither insurance nor funds to cover.

"Yes, that's right," Irene responded to my question. "I want you to pray that there would be no medical attention needed."

"Okay," I said, somewhat reluctantly. I was not reluctant because I doubted God's willingness or power to heal. What I doubted was God's willingness or power to heal *through me*. And it wasn't a psychological dysfunction creating that doubt, like personal insecurity or low self-esteem. It was a spiritual dysfunction.

I had never seen anyone divinely healed. And I had never asked God to heal someone—not really. Sure, I'd included requests for healing in prayers for the sick. But I always couched those prayers in all kinds of caveats. What I was really praying for was peace despite the suffering, healing through modern medicine, comfort and nearness from God's Spirit. But asking God directly to heal someone? Those parts of my prayers amounted to something like, "Oh and of course, God, if you're up for it—which I assume you're not—but if you're up for it and want to do all the work of divine healing with no faith or participation on the part of the ailing or the healthy, then we'd welcome that too."

What was both troubling and enlivening about Irene's request was that she seemed to have real faith for healing. She had expectation; I'd only ever had openness. She also seemed to assume I knew how to pray for healing. But I hadn't the first idea where to start. So I did what plenty of pastors do in this type of situation. I faked it.

I laid my hand over Irene's eyes and acknowledged that the healing of the body is an aspect of Jesus' coming Kingdom. I asked for Jesus' Kingdom to come in Irene's eyes. And I prayed a simple, brief prayer in Jesus' name that during the presurgery consult appointment later that week there would be "no medical attention needed."

The following Sunday a visibly excited Irene came up to me before worship began.

"Pastor, I met with the ophthalmologist and he said, 'Well, Irene, this is surprising but fantastic news. Your condition has dramatically changed somehow since I saw you last week, and there will be no medical attention needed.' He used that very phrase!"

Irene was elated. I was stunned. But, again, I'm a pastor, so I faked it. I smiled and hugged her and gave thanks to God, as if this was just another miracle story in the everyday life of the everlasting Kingdom.

That's a spectacular story and I share it to draw your attention not to the spectacle but to the problem. I had attended church regularly since childhood, served in a variety of lay leadership roles, earned a biblical degree, worked in a number of vocational ministry roles, received thorough ongoing pastoral training, and planted a church. I somehow made it through all that without ever once praying for the sort of miracle that peppers the New Testament.

How could that be? How could someone like me receive so much pastoral training and never be given a healthy model for supernatural practice? And I'm not trying to pass the buck here, either, as if this was just a failure of my teachers and leaders. Equally troubling is the fact that I had read Scripture prayerfully every morning for approximately half my life at that point—particularly the Gospels where Jesus heals frequently and likewise sends his disciples out to heal. And never once had I given healing prayer a real shot.

Many faithful followers of Jesus today are held back in the ministry of the Spirit not by a lack of desire but by a lack of practice. We do not know how. We do not know where to start. We believe God speaks today, heals today, delivers today, but no one has ever given us a healthy model for practice.

Part 3 of this book aims to fill that void, offering practical instruction on the use of common New Testament expressions of an ordinary life empowered by the Spirit of the living God: discernment, prophecy, healing, witness, and redemptive suffering.

THEOLOGY, MODEL, AND PRACTICE

John Wimber, founder of the Vineyard movement, formulated a helpful maxim that goes something like this: For anything to be picked up off the pages of Scripture and lived in a local community within a particular context, you'll need a *theology*, a *model*, and a *practice*.[1]

We must have a *theology*, meaning a common understanding of what Scripture teaches about a particular topic. Theology must be rock solid, and the shared belief about the teaching of Scripture should be common across various church communities, traditions, and contexts. Sadly, that is not always the case, but it should be.

Then we need a *model*, a shared way of expression for that common belief here and now—among this community and in this place. A model is not infallible. It is simply the contextual work of any disciple-maker, translating the expression of a belief in a way that fits a people and a place. For instance, the way teaching (a gift of the Spirit according to the letters of Paul) is expressed varies across communities and traditions.

Some traditions, most notably Catholics and many mainline Protestant denominations, offer a homily, which is a brief reflection on a biblical passage. Evangelicals, however, typically offer a long-form teaching meant to persuade and sanctify the congregation. Which group has the right model? Neither. There's liberty in the expression of the gift based on the needs of the congregation. We share the imperative of making disciples of Jesus, and the most effective way the teaching of Scripture serves that end among these people in this place is the right model. The ministry of the Holy Spirit, plain on the pages of Scripture, often feels entirely inaccessible to the modern, everyday Jesus follower because we lack a coherent model. "Of course I believe God heals today, but have I ever prayed with confidence for God's miraculous healing power? Well, no. I don't know how."

Finally, we must have space to *practice*, meaning safe space created within a local church community where it is okay to fail and learn the mechanics of that model together. Practice in an individual's craft has mastery as its end goal. In his bestselling book *Outliers*, Malcolm Gladwell popularized the 10,000 hour rule, pointing to a number of success stories in which 10,000 hours of practice at a given craft led to mastery.

But that is *absolutely not* what I mean by "practice."

Practice, in the sense we're talking about, should be understood in the context of a team. When a team of any kind gathers to practice—a dance team preparing for a performance, a basketball team getting ready for a game, or a band rehearsing for a recital—the unspoken agreement is that mistakes are okay and perfection is not demanded. Practice is protected space where the stakes are lowered because it's not the performance, game, or recital. Instead, we are working together so that we all grow together through shared practice. *That* is the definition of practice I have in mind—one aimed not at individual mastery but more mature, shared ministry.

Practice is where the most liberty lies; it's the most frequently overlooked aspect of the Spirit's ministry. To return to the teaching example, if someone within the local church I lead indicated that they were gifted in teaching, I wouldn't respond, "Great! You should preach from the pulpit next Sunday!" There must be space given for an individual to develop that teaching gift where the stakes are lower, and most modern churches understand this implicitly—training up lay teachers in classes, small groups, and similar gatherings. However, when it comes to the other gifts of the Spirit, like prophecy or healing, for example, most churches do not have space for practice. This creates the false belief that a gift of healing is for the uber-anointed world traveler and prophecy is for the holy weirdo with dreams and visions rather than the ordinary disciple in the local church. If we want today's churches to look like the ancient churches that set the world on fire, we must practice as those early communities practiced. We do this through setting aside intentional spaces of training in the various gifts and expressions of the Spirit, which are designed to form us into empty channels through which the Spirit's power flows on earth as in heaven.

The five expressions in the chapters that follow are obviously not exhaustive. Rather, each expression is one that is common in the New Testament church and uncommon in the modern, Western church. Additionally, each of the expressions of the Spirit is also one for which I can offer both a firm foundation of theological study and a wealth of experience in healthy, time-tested practice. I have elected to omit the expressions of the Spirit for which I lack one or both of these criteria.

The aim is to offer a firm biblical foundation, a suggested model, and clear, instructive practice to equip the saints for works of service, as Paul writes to the Ephesians.[2] While mature practice of some expressions of Holy Spirit–empowered ministry requires a community embracing practice together, individual practices are offered to close each of these chapters, offering a starting place for anyone, anywhere.

The aim of these chapters is

1. to awaken within you a desire to know God in all the ways he has made himself knowable—including those that may be unfamiliar to your experience but common to biblical experience;
2. to lay a firm biblical foundation under your feet that you can stand on confidently with your desire for more of God; and, finally,
3. to offer you a clear way of practice for exercising and growing in each of the expressions of Holy Spirit ministry.

We cannot experience God in new ways with our noses in a book. We must get our feet beyond the boundaries of our comfort zones and get our hands dirty in the practice of the Spirit's power. That's what part 3 is—an instruction manual for practice.

SEVEN

DISCERNMENT

Dear friends, do not believe every spirit, but test the spirits to
see whether they are from God, because many false prophets
have gone out into the world.

1 JOHN 4:1

"HEY MAN, I KNOW THIS SOUNDS CRAZY, but I'm calling on
behalf of our elder board to see if you'd want my job."

I started laughing. "John Mark, you know there's no way I'm
going anywhere!"

My friend John Mark Comer was calling me on a Sunday
afternoon in April 2020. I was happily leading the church I'd
helped plant in Brooklyn, delighting in the deep friendships that
had grown up around us over our twelve years in New York City,
and I had every intention of giving the rest of my life in faithful
service to that community.

"I know. I told them you'd say that," John Mark said. "Will
you please just pray about it for one week before you tell me
absolutely not?"

A few days later, I took a prayer walk.

"Okay God, I'm gonna walk for an hour, and if you want to talk to me about this Portland thing, I'm listening."

Almost immediately, God began to reframe my thinking. I had been seeing John Mark's invitation in terms of uprooting my family and my plans. But as I prayed, God put an image of a plant in my mind, along with a phrase focused on my wife: "Plant Kirsten in soil where she'd flourish."

On that prayer walk, I sensed that God had selected Portland as the place where he would reawaken dormant parts of Kirsten—character traits from her teenage self she'd deferred (even unknowingly) to live *my dream* alongside me.

I didn't immediately tell Kirsten about this, but I held on to it prayerfully.

One thing led to another, and I said yes to a trip to Portland to explore the possibility of becoming the lead pastor of Bridgetown Church.

At what I felt was God's invitation, I journaled a few prayers the day before we left for Portland—very specific requests—and said, "Alright Lord, if you're calling me to pastor Bridgetown Church, answer these prayers clearly and directly during the week we spend in Portland. If you don't, I can't do this. It's just too big a decision to make without you speaking clearly and emphatically."

One of those prayers was that Kirsten would feel parts of herself reawakening during our trip, as I'd sensed on that prayer walk. A second prayer was that the leadership of Bridgetown would possess not merely a willingness to put up with my radical commitment to prayer but a shared desire for the same.

After arriving in Portland, Kirsten and I were relaxing and talking before heading to a dinner with some Bridgetown Church staff and elders. During a lull in the conversation, Kirsten offered a passing comment: "You know what's strange? Since the moment our flight landed, I keep thinking about myself in high school, even feeling like my teenage self. I wonder . . . if we actually do this, will God reawaken old parts of me I've forgotten? Not sure why I'm thinking about that. So interesting."

"Huh," I responded. "That *is* interesting . . ."

A few hours later at the dinner, a Bridgetown elder named Peter said to me, "So, John Mark tells us you're really into prayer."

"Yeah," I said, moving through the buffet table and scooping food onto my plate. "I mean, I am a Christian pastor, so you'd hope so, right?"

"Well, have you ever heard of this group called 24-7 Prayer?"

"Sure have." I'd just been appointed national director of that very organization, though it was not yet public knowledge. No one at the dinner had any idea.

Peter continued, "I really like what they're doing. If you come here, would you be open to bringing that kind of culture with you?"

"Yeah," I smiled. "I'm open to that."

To make a long story short, every one of those prayers I'd written was answered within the first twenty-four hours of our time in Portland. God knocked me on my back, and I can honestly say that in the year following the decision to move, I experienced the constant sense of God's goodness and blessing like never before.

———

Back in Brooklyn, I worked alongside a pastor named Zach. We were close friends before we were coworkers, and it was amazing to serve together. A couple years before I moved to Portland, Zach lived a nearly identical discernment process.

Lindsay, his wife, was increasingly coming alive spiritually, discovering new vocational desires that were more in line with her unique gifting. She applied to an exclusive graduate program in San Francisco that would open up new opportunities—and she got in. Zach had long-term ministry desires that aligned perfectly with a family of churches in the Bay Area. Sensing an invitation from the Lord, he reached out and doors began to open for him too.

Before long, Zach and Lindsay said tearful goodbyes to the church community they helped plant and the friends who'd become like family. And, like Abraham and Sarah, they moved cross-country on an adventure from God.

But things didn't go as planned. I still remember Zach's phone call a few months after their move. He hadn't been able to find a ministry position, so he was a barista by morning and stay-at-home dad all afternoon. Lindsay's program was underwhelming, and life got so hard and money so tight she elected not to complete the degree. Zach didn't work in full-time vocational ministry again for approximately five years, a window within which they moved back to his hometown after the sudden and tragic loss of his mother.

God knocked them on their backs with his clear voice, and they followed in radical obedience. And what followed was not a season of blessing but of suffering.

So what do we make of that? Did God will a season of suffering? And if he did, why didn't he just say that up front? They would have followed him anywhere, and maybe knowing they were walking off a cliff would've made the freefall a little more bearable. But how are you supposed to keep on trusting a God who whispers with a smile when he's leading you into an ambush? Or, scariest of all possibilities, was it *not* God speaking and leading them at all? Were they mistaken about God's voice and direction? If they got this wrong, how could they know for sure if it had ever been God's voice they were hearing?

To hear and live by God's voice, it would seem, is one of the most potent and most dangerous aspects of Christian spirituality. Nothing matters more than learning to discern the voice of God, and yet few things in life are more susceptible to pain, abuse, delusion, and deception. Who among us hasn't cried out to God, and God seemingly says nothing back in the waiting? Who among us hasn't been hurt by the misuse of God's Word by an authority figure? *And* who among us hasn't been enlivened by the still, small whisper of God's voice we learn increasingly as we follow the Good Shepherd? Who among us hasn't known the blessing of the first story, and who among us hasn't endured the pain, confusion—even abandonment—of the second?

PRUDENT MONEY CHANGERS

Fourth-century monk John Cassian said one of the primary works of spiritual maturity is to become an increasingly "prudent money changer."[1] In the Roman Empire of his time, counterfeit coins were common. Money changers had to become so familiar with the real thing that if someone dropped a counterfeit in their hands, they could immediately identify it as a fake—by the weight, the engraving, the metal. Like a money changer who became intimately familiar with every aspect of a genuine coin, we must grow so familiar with God's voice that we can recognize a counterfeit and recognize it quickly. That's discernment.

Both Paul and John, who authored much of the New Testament, write about discernment, describing it as both a gift and a practice. But despite its frequency on the pages of Scripture, discernment has gone, for the most part, without comment in the modern church, relegated to the mysterious or overlooked. Jesuit priest and author Thomas Green notes, "The art of discernment is both central to the Christian life today and, at the same time, not very well understood even by prayerful and committed Christians."[2]

Discernment is the gift and practice of attuning to God's voice amid the competing counterfeit noise. This chapter will offer understanding and equip you for growing in discernment both individually and in community. To get there we must begin by acknowledging the competing voices vying for our attention: God's whisper and the deceiver's weeds.

GOD'S WHISPER

On the evening of resurrection Sunday, rumors were swirling about the empty tomb where Jesus' body had been laid to rest. Two disciples were walking from Jerusalem to Emmaus, and the resurrected Lord himself began to walk alongside them. While they walked, Jesus preached the first resurrection sermon in history—and they didn't even notice he was the guy who'd been resurrected.

When the two travelers arrived at their journey's end, *"Jesus continued on as if he were going farther."*[3] Was this just a charade, or would the risen Lord really have been content to spend the first Easter Sunday with a couple of people who never even realized who he was? If this were an isolated event, I guess you could come to either conclusion. But this isn't an isolated event.

Rewind the biblical story all the way back to 1 Kings 19. Elijah had literally prayed fire down from heaven, but now he was a wanted man. After forty days as a fugitive, he climbed Mount Horeb to cry out to God. Elijah must've made the ascent with great expectation. After all, this was the same mountain Moses had climbed all those years ago to receive the Ten Commandments. And now Elijah *needed* to hear from God—the God who sent the fire, the God who wrote on the stone tablets, the God whose glory left Moses' face aglow. So Elijah went to the site to say, "Speak to me, Lord. Here I am!" And sure enough . . .

> The LORD said, "Go out and stand on the mountain in the presence of the LORD, for the LORD is about to pass by." Then a great and powerful wind tore the mountains apart and shattered the rocks before the LORD, but the LORD was not in the wind. After the wind there was an earthquake, but the LORD was not in the earthquake. After the earthquake came a fire, but the LORD was not in the fire. And after the fire came a gentle whisper. When Elijah heard it, he pulled his cloak over his face.[4]

A gentle whisper, famously translated by the King James Version of the Bible as "a still, small voice." But the phrase I want to draw your attention to isn't the iconic one. It's the one most tend to overlook. "Go out and stand on the mountain in the presence of the LORD, for *the LORD is about to pass by.*"[5]

Interesting, huh? It's that same phrase from Emmaus hundreds of years later. The plot thickens if you rewind even further to the Moses moment Elijah was reliving on this very mountain: "Then the LORD said, 'There is a place near me where you may stand on a rock. When my glory *passes by,* I will put you in a cleft in the rock and cover you with my hand until I have *passed by.*'"[6] This is, arguably, the peak moment of intimacy in the whole of the Old Testament, and there that phrase is again: *God passing by.*

And not long before his walk on the road to Emmaus, Jesus took another walk—this one on water: "Shortly before dawn he went out to them, walking on the lake. *He was about to pass by them.*"[7] There's that phrase again.

So just to be clear, Jesus, you were really willing just to stroll across the waves right next to their boat unnoticed and meet them the next morning at the shore? It certainly seems like it.

Drag all that history with you back to the road to Emmaus. The same Jesus, content to walk on water right past the disciples in the boat, seems content to walk alongside these two unnamed disciples all the way to Emmaus and pass right by.

"But they urged him strongly, 'Stay with us, for it is nearly evening; the day is almost over.' So he went in to stay with them."[8] Over dinner they finally recognized Jesus and noted that their hearts had been burning within them all along the road as they talked with Jesus.[9] And the rest, as they say, is history.

My point is that even on the pages of the Bible, God's native language is a whisper, and a whisper is hard to hear and easy to ignore. What if God is speaking to you far more than you realize? What if the majority of divine instructions or encounters in your life to date are missed connections—magic moments that could have been, but the Lord passed right by you?

We tend to miss God in our midst, not because he's too extraordinary but because he's too ordinary. We tend to look for God in the wind, earthquake, and fire rather than the whisper. We climb our own Mount Horebs with expectation—when that preacher speaks, when I attend this conference or worship experience, when I go on my upcoming silent retreat—pigeonholing God's voice into special times and places. But all the while, he's "about to pass by."

What if you could know him not just at the table in the evening but all the way along the road to Emmaus? What if you could hear him not just on top of Mount Horeb but in the valley of suffering? Pete Greig writes, "If we are ever to feel fully safe and truly loved by the Lord of all the earth, we must eventually—like Elijah on Horeb and that couple on the Emmaus road—learn to listen for his voice in the anticlimax of life's nonevents."[10]

WHY DOESN'T GOD YELL?

All of this raises an obvious question: Why doesn't God yell? Why play it so coy? The answer to that inquiry is equally clear in the biblical story: Because when God does speak in the most obvious, undeniable ways, it's relatively ineffective.

Elijah's fire spectacle didn't seem to do much good. It led to a manhunt, not a revival. Jesus' miracles seemed only subjectively effective, meaning it was up to the eyes and ears of the onlooking crowd to recognize God's activity in the miracles rather than explain them away. Even the empty tomb didn't lead immediately to widespread revival but to persecution, imprisonment, and public lashings for everyone who dared to believe.

So maybe God whispers not because he's evasive but because he's intimate. Because the louder his voice gets, the more polarizing he becomes—some want to make use of his power for their vision (like the disciples who planned the size and location of their thrones in his Kingdom) and others want to dismiss his power to hold on to the illusion of their control (like the priests who had so much prestige to surrender if Jesus was really King). Maybe God whispers because it's the only way he can get what he wants most, what was lost in Eden: to walk with you and me in familiar intimacy that we might know God as he truly is and discover ourselves as we truly are in his presence.

THE DECEIVER'S WEEDS

In Matthew 13, Jesus paints the picture of a rich wheat field. A crafty enemy invades this field at night, sowing weeds. The owner of the field then elects to allow both the weeds and wheat to grow together because the removal of the weeds would surely damage the wheat. Instead, he decides to separate the weeds from the wheat at harvest time.

Jesus explains this parable as a depiction of the harvest at the end of the age. However, it's also a helpful metaphor for the inner world of the individual, where weeds and wheat grow together. Your inner world is naturally a rowdy room filled with competing voices. The voice of God is active and present in your inner life, but there are other voices vying for your attention too. One of the reasons it's difficult to hear God's voice is because he's got a lot of competition. It's hard to hear a whisper amid all that noise.

There really is an indwelling Holy Spirit speaking life, clarity, and direction into the life of every believer and producing a rich harvest in the soul. And there really is a deceptive enemy, scheming in the night to sow lies and confusion into the life of every believer and spoiling (or at the very least choking and diminishing) the harvest in my soul and yours.

To ignore the role of the devil who sows weeds in the night

is to attempt to bring about a rich harvest from my inner life without cultivating the soil. To obsess over the devil, blaming our spiritual enemy for every stubbed toe and twist of fate, is to ignore the flesh and the world, again attempting to bring about a rich harvest from my inner life without cultivating the soil. Rather than ignoring or obsessing over the devil, we should "test the spirits to see whether they are from God," in the words of the apostle John.[11]

Because the inner life of the believer is like the field that contains both God's wheat and the enemy's weeds, the process of hearing and keeping in step with the Spirit involves attentiveness to the inner dynamics and movements of the soul. The Spirit's whisper is directed at the soul's depths, while the deceiver's lies appeal to the shallow waters of the ego.

THE EGO AND THE SOUL

You and I are forever tempted toward self-absorption. We imagine ourselves at the center of the story, and in so doing we dethrone Jesus and confuse the voice of the Good Shepherd with an imposter. What is broadly known today as "the ego" Scripture most often names "the flesh." The flesh is where competing desires take root within the individual person, getting all the way into our personality structure and thought patterns—ambition, insecurity, perfectionism, and the like. All of these are not bad on their own, but they do serve as competing voices to the Spirit's whisper. For example, a propensity toward ambition may make hearing a call to a more hidden, uncelebrated role more difficult for a driven individual to recognize as the Spirit's voice offering life.

These sorts of deeply ingrained sin patterns are most commonly summarized as "the ego": that invisible internal world of shallow desire that feels good to gratify in the immediate but undignifies and dehumanizes over time. The deceiver is the most experienced of con artists, familiar with our individual personality structures, vices, and weak points.

Scripture also teaches that when our spiritual enemy fails to deceive us as an angel of darkness, he comes instead disguised as an angel of light, meaning that when we lose a taste for temptation toward obvious sins, the deceiver doesn't give up but shifts his strategy.[12] Saint Ignatius expounds, "It is a mark of the evil spirit to assume the appearance of an angel of light. He begins by suggesting thoughts that are suited to a devout soul, and ends by suggesting his own."[13]

The enemy of your soul gladly nudges you toward standing on stages leading worship, working in impoverished villages digging wells, or sitting around church leadership tables making decisions—so long as he can magnify your ego under the clever disguise of pious spirituality. He is equally content with guiding you to a brothel or to a prayer meeting—so long as the result is to feed and strengthen your ego rather than your soul.

When my ego becomes the ear I'm listening with, even my spiritual life can devolve into narcissism focused on "me," not "Thee." Worship becomes a quest for experiential self-fulfillment, obedience is traded for gratifying personal dreams and passions, spiritual practices are diluted into methods of personal wellness. And the aim of discipleship—to become like Christ, a gift of others-centered love freely given—gets subtly replaced by new goals of spiritual thrill-seeking or personal peace.

The same principle that holds with the inflation of the ego applies to a deflation of the ego. When the devil hits a roadblock in tempting you toward obvious sin, he doesn't give up. He changes his strategy, trying to stall or slow your progress by guilt, shame, or scrupulosity—the evaluation and perfection of your own spiritual life—leading to anxiety and self-focus.

The key to discerning between the Holy Spirit's whisper and the deceiver's scheme, then, starts with recognizing what the voice is doing to you as you listen to it. What part of you is being inflamed by this inner voice—your shallow hungers or your deep longings, your ego or your soul? Discernment is, in large part, the spiritual practice of differentiating between the listening ear of your ego and your soul.

God appeals to the deepest longings within us. The deceiver appeals to our shallow hungers. God nourishes the soul. The deceiver massages the ego. Become a prudent money changer, to return to Cassian's image. Grow so familiar with God's whisper you can tell a counterfeit and tell it quickly.

The big mistake most sincere apprentices make when it comes to discernment is treating it like a prescription, something taken temporarily to deal with a specific issue, instead of a vitamin, something taken daily to maintain good health. They act as if discernment is reserved for life's major decisions—a cross-country move, a career change, or a marriage proposal. But if we haven't learned the Spirit's whisper in the day-to-day, discernment in life's major decisions is mostly just a charade where we'll follow God's direction if he puts a billboard on the highway reading, "Marry Casey. She really is the one." Otherwise we pray a few times, then do what seems best to us—which isn't bad, but neither is it discernment. Ruth Haley Barton says that the practice of discernment "recognize[s] and respond[s] to the presence and activity of God—both in the ordinary moments and in the larger decisions of our lives."[14]

We could also say that discernment is less like decoding a message and more like learning a new language, a dialect that we grow more comfortable and natural with the more we listen and interact with a native speaker. Fill your ordinary, daily life with the regular practice of discernment, and that'll make the Spirit's whisper in the big, pressure-packed decisions a language you can hear.

Discernment is a gift of the Spirit, practiced individually and within community, by which I mean that learning God's voice essentially involves both.

DISCERNMENT IN COMMUNITY

No individual has a completely accurate self-perception or a perfect read on their own inner dynamics and motivations. Reaching all the way back to Eden, life in communion with God has always involved living in community with others, and attunement to God's voice has always required community in order to mature to its full potential.

Author and spiritual director Jared Patrick Boyd says, "Discernment in community means that we're doing the work of noticing and nurturing the presence of God's activity with and for one another."[15] The way we do that, practically speaking, comes through three types of relationships: spiritual friendship, spiritual direction, and formal group discernment.

Spiritual friendship

On a recent Sunday evening, after preaching three times at our church's various worship gatherings across the city, I was tired and hungry as I sat down at a Vietnamese restaurant across from my close friend Tim. We immediately started negotiating a joint food order we'd share over the next hour or two.

Tim and I text often, go on hiking adventures, and hang out with our families, who are in similar life stages. We have fun together. But these Sunday nights are different. They're intentional. Tim and I share a joint passion for increasingly living in response to the Spirit's whisper—and for eating from as many of our city's great restaurants as possible. We call this monthly tradition the "Portland Sunday Supper Club."

On this particular Sunday evening, as we loaded vermicelli noodles and lemongrass chicken onto our plates, Tim said, "I remember you sharing with me last month about God really turning your attention to your marriage. How's that been going?" Later that night, a pile of plates between us and the check on the table waiting to be paid, we looked around and realized we were the last customers left in the restaurant. We'd shared vulnerably, listened deeply, asked questions aimed to deepen one another's attention to God, and occasionally offered each other direction. This is spiritual friendship—intentionally inviting another person into your sense of the Spirit's whisper and asking that they refine your attention and response.

Spiritual friendship can be practiced between two friends or as a group. It involves deep, prayerful listening and asking questions more often than offering direction or advice. It demands deep trust and complete vulnerability, and it can only be experienced between people with a shared commitment to (and existing practice of) individual discernment.

Spiritual direction

I have been seeing the same spiritual director for more than five years now. In our monthly appointments I have laughed, wept, and had many breakthrough moments of clarity. Spiritual direction is more formal than spiritual friendship, practiced individually with a qualified sacred listener. When searching for a spiritual director, seek out a seasoned believer who is well-trained in the art of holy listening and committed to local church community. Because discernment matures in community, beware of a spiritual director who is untethered to a church community and fostering their own ongoing process of maturing spiritually.

Formal group discernment

Finally, for major decisions, formal group discernment can be helpful. Once a quarter, Kirsten and I break bread with our "discernment team," which includes four respected spiritual advisers who see our life together from different but equally important perspectives. These are people who know the kind of spouse, parent, and friend Kirsten and I each want to be. They know our personality quirks and shadow sides.

Over dinner we share all the major ministry opportunities for the next quarter. Whether it's traveling to preach, contributing to a larger ministry project, or even writing this book—all such activities are discerned in community. Formal group discernment is a chosen constraint that helps me and my family keep in step with the Spirit.

I will never reach a stage of spiritual maturity that allows me to practice discernment independently of community. Spiritual friendship, spiritual direction, and formal group discernment are not training wheels that I'll one day take off the bike when I'm really ready to ride. They're lifelong commitments. And that is not because God is playing it coy. It's because, to borrow the words of Genesis, "It is not good for a human to be alone."[16] We are meant to know and hear God within the context of community.

DISCERNMENT INDIVIDUALLY

If you rewind Elijah's story—before the still, small whisper on Mount Horeb, even before the divine fire on Mount Carmel— you'll discover a seemingly random event that I believe allows us to watch a biblical prophet being trained in the art of discernment:

> Then the word of the LORD came to Elijah: "Leave here, turn eastward and hide in the Kerith Ravine, east of the Jordan. You will drink from the brook, and I have directed the ravens to supply you with food there."[17]

For context, Israel was experiencing political corruption, foreign occupation, and oppression. And amid all that very urgent need for divine help, God told Elijah to go live on his own in the wilderness, drinking from a brook and getting his groceries delivered by ravens. This was an invitation to wild, costly, surrendered obedience that, at the same time, seemed entirely unproductive. Living as a raven-dependent hermit in no way addressed the corruption, occupation, and oppression that Elijah (and presumably God) was so concerned about.

But Elijah did it—lived by the brook, ate from the ravens. He said yes to God. God proved faithful. And none of it seemed all that immediately productive.

I should also mention that in the first verse of this very chapter, Elijah had, at God's direction, prophesied a multiple-year drought in the land. So when God sent Elijah to live by a water source that was *dependent on rain*, you can probably guess what happened next: "Some time later the brook dried up because there had been no rain in the land."[18]

The story continues, "Then the word of the LORD came to him: 'Go at once to Zarephath in the region of Sidon and stay there. I have directed a widow there to supply you with food.'"[19] When Elijah gets to this widow's house, she has no food. God works through Elijah to miraculously fill her cupboards and supernaturally heal her son. So, from Elijah's perspective, God is speaking to him, he's radically obeying, and the results are occasionally miraculous but just as often seemingly unproductive in terms of the core issue—corruption, occupation, and oppression.

The defining question of Elijah's early years is this: Would God do all this just so Elijah could learn his voice? So Elijah would trust God enough to call down fire on Carmel? So Elijah would know God deeply enough to search for him while alone in the wilderness yet again on the other side of the miraculous fire? It certainly seems to me that God was putting his heart in Elijah before he poured his power through Elijah. By the brook God taught him dependence and trust. At the house, God taught him compassion for the widow and the fatherless.

Author and professor Bobby Clinton argues that both Scripture and church history indicate that pretty much everything God speaks to us until around our sixties is preparation. If there's fruit, that's a bonus, but the aim is preparation and training in discernment—to learn God's voice and live with such radical trust that your life becomes an open channel between heaven and earth.[20]

God's whisper tends to be equal parts enlivening and terrifying, resonating deeply in our souls while also requiring risk. We never achieve a stage of discipleship where God's voice becomes comfort without trepidation, all blessing and no cost, fruit without risk. We never graduate from this. Elijah didn't, and neither do we. Listening to and living by God's voice is less a method and more a radical commitment to terrifying obedience and a stubborn willingness to risk foolishness. Elijah's story reveals the two steps forward, one step back experiential process of a biblical prophet learning to discern God's voice amid the cacophony of noise that is the world, the flesh, and the devil.

Discernment is the school of listening to and living by God's voice, and as long as we are living in a contested world, there's no graduating from this school. If we are going to ask God for his fire to fall, we must equally be willing to allow God to train us in perceiving his voice amid all the competing noise.

THE GRACE OF DISCERNMENT

Discernment is not a maze God puts us in or a puzzle for us to solve. It's a gift of the Spirit allowing us to be led by the Good Shepherd who knows and loves us. To return to where we began the chapter, God didn't trick Zach and Lindsay. Nor did they make some error they had to make up for. In their lives, as in my own, they discovered again and again that their hope lies not in perfectly walking God's path, but in God, the guide himself, who is always coming after us—not with a stick to punish but with grace to guide us home.

PRACTICE: EXAMEN

The Prayer of Examen (or the "examination of conscience") is a way of prayer developed by Saint Ignatius. Praying the Examen typically involves five steps:

1. **Gratitude:** Note the ways you have experienced God's loving presence today and thank the Giver for his gifts.
2. **Ask:** Invite the Spirit to provide insight beyond human capacity.
3. **Review:** Review the day you've just lived in partnership with the Spirit, noting the experiences of God's nearness while also checking for the invitations you may have missed—moments when God passed right by, unnoticed or ignored.
4. **Repentance:** Ask forgiveness for any moments you rejected, ignored, or rebelled against God's invitation to you.
5. **Renewal:** Looking ahead to the next twenty-four hours, resolve to live in concert with God's direction.

Note that this prayer involves attunement to the inner life—mind, will, and emotions. It demands attentiveness to the whole person and cultivates emotional maturity as you review your day in terms of your thoughts, feelings, and motives.

I practice the Examen daily on my commute home from work. As I cycle down the street, I pray aloud, speaking directly to my Father in heaven. I savor the day's blessings, recount my day with the Spirit's introspective aid, ask forgiveness, and pray intercession as God's mercy goes behind and before me.

They say hindsight is 20/20, and that certainly applies to the way we navigate our spirituality. It's easier to perceive God's presence when we're looking back than it is in the moment. Praying the Examen is the practice of recognizing God in hindsight. It's the practice of remembering when, on this day, our hearts were burning as he walked alongside us.

And as we learn to recognize God in hindsight, the most amazing thing happens. Slowly but surely, we learn to recognize God in the present—to know him not just at the dinner table in the evening but all along the road to Emmaus, to recognize him in those moments when "the Lord is about to pass by."

EIGHT

PROPHECY

Follow the way of love and eagerly desire gifts of the Spirit,
especially prophecy.

1 CORINTHIANS 14:1

"EXCUSE ME, MISS? I'm sorry to interrupt, but I believe I have a
word for you. Do you mind if I share it?"

We were in the middle of a church prayer meeting, and Gavin
interrupted the prayer with a request directed not to God but to
Emi, the woman next to him. Startled, Emi looked up.

Gavin continued, now that he had her attention, "As we were
praying I had a picture of an abacus, and as I asked the Lord about
it, I felt he was highlighting you. Do you mind if I share it?" (An
abacus, if you're not familiar, is like an old-fashioned calculator,
with metal rods and sliding beads set in a frame.)

I had known Emi for years but Gavin was new to me. He
was a friend of a friend who happened to be visiting Brooklyn for
the weekend, and he'd tagged along with this friend to our prayer
meeting. He was a complete stranger to just about everyone in
that room.

Emi, on the other hand, had been committed to our church for nearly the entire three years of its existence. And she had been our interim children's ministry coordinator for about six months, offering her evening and weekend hours to pull off a Sunday kids' program. Two weeks earlier I'd offered Emi a permanent position. She'd respectfully responded, "I'd like to think it over." But in reality, at that point she had no intention of making the ministry position permanent—she had a great full-time gig in the nonprofit world with a window office, upward mobility, and a supervisor who'd already promoted her once.

But as she prayed in the coming days, Emi began to feel a strange pull from God to leave her burgeoning career behind and become a part-time children's ministry coordinator at a church plant. She knew it was ludicrous. This was New York City. A decent full-time salary with benefits gets you a shared room in an asbestos-infested apartment building. A part-time position at a church plant that survives exclusively on donations? That's absurd. But she couldn't shake the sense that God was saying, "This is where I'm leading you. *Follow me, and I'll take care of the rest.*"

I learned all of this after the fact. But that's the context for when Gavin, the out-of-town visitor, interrupted an otherwise ordinary prayer meeting.

"I saw this picture of an abacus," Gavin went on, "and all the beads were moved to one side. I have a sense, and I think it may be from God, that you are contemplating a major decision and every bit of human wisdom is telling you to choose the option that's clearly safer. But God is saying, 'Go for the option with all the risk—the empty side of the equation. That's where I'm leading you. *Follow me, and I'll take care of the rest.*'"

Gavin repeated that line verbatim to what Emi had been hearing God whisper to her in prayer. She didn't respond verbally, just nodded her head in the affirmative as tears began streaming down her face.

And that's how Emi ended up discipling a bunch of kids at Oaks Church Brooklyn: prophecy. She can explain her beliefs with nothing but Scripture, but she cannot tell her story apart from the voice of God speaking to her through someone else. The foundation of her life is biblical truth, but the shape of her life is prophetic.

The Spirit-empowered ministry of prophecy means hearing and speaking a message from God that is directed to another individual or group. In this chapter we will examine what prophecy means biblically, communally, and practically.

PROPHECY IN THE BIBLE

Put simply, there is no era of biblical history without the prophetic. Apart from prophecy, the biblical story is one that can't be told.

In the beginning, God spoke creation into being. Sun, moon, and stars; land and sea; magnolia trees, wild ferns, and rose bushes; red-breasted robins, geckos, and stingrays—all of it came into being by the breath (*ruakh*) of God, also known as the Spirit of God. When God created people as his image bearers, he put his creative breath into them, thereby distinguishing humanity from every other aspect of creation and commissioning them to go on creating.

Then, of course, there's that whole bit about the forbidden fruit. Human beings were always meant to be filled with God's Spirit, but sin stole God's breath from our lungs. Throughout the rest of the Old Testament, God's strategy for redemption mimics his strategy for creation. Against the ravages of sin, God keeps speaking, re-creating the same way he created—through his breath, his Spirit.

Numbers 11 records a key moment in the unfolding story of

the prophetic. "Then the LORD came down in the cloud and spoke with [Moses], and he took some of the power of the Spirit that was on him and put it on the seventy elders. When the Spirit rested on them, they prophesied—but did not do so again."[1]

When the presence of God fell like a cloud on Moses, God spoke. And Moses, in turn, spoke the words of God to the people. Prophecy, remember, is hearing and speaking a message from God that is directed to another person. And when some of that same Spirit was given to the seventy elders, they all began to prophesy. But, as the passage states, it was short-lived. It was not an ongoing gift; it was a divine moment.

This passage exemplifies an Old Testament pattern: God selected certain people and communicated with them directly, and those people then shared the private whispers of God publicly. These people were called prophets. But they were the exception, not the rule. The good news was that God was speaking. The bad news was that prophecy was relatively rare.

But there is a telling moment at the close of Numbers 11, where Moses says: "I wish that all the Lord's people were prophets and that the Lord would put his Spirit on them!"[2] Moses realized that his experience of God's nearness was the exception, not the rule. The very best of what he was experiencing from God wasn't common. Moses' longing points ahead to the same Spirit speaking prophetically to and through everyone in the community.

That Old Testament pattern continued until the Son, who is the Word of God, took on human form and became known as Jesus of Nazareth. John poetically claims that the life of Jesus is a living, breathing prophecy.[3] And after his resurrection, Jesus appeared to his disciples and reenacted God's creation of man and woman in the beginning: "And with that he breathed on them and said, 'Receive the Holy Spirit.'"[4] Essentially he said, "Here's my breath for your lungs, my *ruakh*, my Spirit."

Keep turning to the right in your Bible and you'll come to the book of Acts, where the church was born on the day of Pentecost with the promised gift of the Holy Spirit. Immediately after the Spirit was given, all the recipients in the upper room began speaking the words of God. All the Lord's people started acting like prophets—just as Moses had longed for in Numbers 11. And Peter connected this astounding new development to what the prophet Joel had long ago said was coming: "I will pour out my Spirit on all people. Your sons and daughters will prophesy, your old men will dream dreams, your young men will see visions. Even on my servants, both men and women, I will pour out my Spirit in those days."[5]

What was sensational on the day of Pentecost became ordinary as the church matured. Joel's Old Testament prophecy, repeated in Acts by Peter, matured into Paul's New Testament instruction: "Follow the way of love and eagerly desire gifts of the Spirit, especially prophecy . . . the one who prophesies speaks to people for their strengthening, encouraging and comfort."[6]

Paul goes on to write, "I would like every one of you . . . to prophecy,"[7] an echo of Moses from Numbers 11. All of you? Yes, because *all of you* have been filled with the Holy Spirit. *All of you* now permanently carry what the prophets of old had at particular times for particular purposes. That's why this gift is called "prophecy" in the New Testament. It is the ordinary practice of what was extraordinary before the risen Jesus breathed on all of us.

I hope it's becoming clear that prophecy is not an optional subpoint in the biblical story. It's at its very heart. And it should be at the very heart of each of our stories today. If the foundation of our lives is biblical truth, the shape of our lives should be prophetic.

PROPHECY IN COMMUNITY

First Corinthians 14 is the biblical manifesto on the role of prophecy in the local church, the heart of which can be drawn out in three words: "ordinary," "intimacy," and "Jesus."

Prophecy is the ordinary experience of church life.

In 1 Corinthians (and the rest of the New Testament), the assumption is that when God's people gather, God is speaking through us to one another. Prophetic practice in the gathered church is the consistent biblical expectation. Dallas Willard wrote, "If we look at the advice on how the meetings of the church were supposed to proceed as given in 1 Corinthians 14, we see that they assumed that numerous people in the congregation were going to have some kind of communication from God which they would be sharing with others in the group."[8]

It was the first Sunday of my first sabbatical. I was living "in between" in every way imaginable. I'd just said goodbye to the church I planted and people I loved in Brooklyn. I'd said yes to a church I didn't know and people I was yet to meet in Portland. I was an emotional wreck.

I'd retreated into the tropics of Oahu for two months of slowing and processing, but I couldn't slow down. Couldn't stop the wheels turning in my mind that had been racing for the last year. Couldn't stop rehashing conversations I wish I'd done better or differently. Couldn't stop writing sermons in my head, though I had no one to preach to. It was time to rest, and I knew how to slow down my body, but my mind was a different story.

On that Sunday morning, before my family and I headed to a little church down the road where we didn't know anyone, I prayed, "Help. God, I need to hear you. Please help."

I don't remember anything about the music or the preaching at that church, but I do remember this: The pastor got up to give the benediction to close the worship gathering, and this guy who'd been sitting in the back walked up with him. The pastor announced, "Jordan is a trusted leader in our community. He came to me a few minutes ago with a word." He passed the microphone to Jordan, who proceeded to say, "Yeah, you . . ." as he pointed right at me. "I saw you walk in with your family, and through a picture that popped into my mind at that moment I felt God say, 'I've brought this man here to rest, but he doesn't know how to rest. I want to show him.' So if that resonates with you at all, and you're open to it, I'd love to pray for you after we close. If not, please know it was offered humbly in love."

What is that? Just another Sunday. Just the normal experience of church life according to the apostle Paul.

Prophecy invites intimacy.

"His sheep follow him because they know his voice."[9] But of course, for anyone who's ever tried to hear God, we know that our souls aren't automatically attuned to his voice. Experientially, God mostly makes himself available but not obvious, so hearing his voice takes some practice—it takes the uncomfortable risking we call obedience.

How do we learn the Shepherd's voice? We follow him. We ask God to speak to us, then we walk in obedience, only half-sure (at best) that it's God's voice we heard and not our own imagination. Mistakes will be made.

A couple years ago Simon, a friend close enough and respected enough that we named our second son after him, was on the Metro North, a train that carries passengers from Grand Central Station in the heart of Manhattan to the Hudson Valley towns north of the city. He settled in for a two-hour trip across from a woman who Simon guessed worked in business based on her attire. Simon was pretty sure he felt God whisper a prophetic word related to this stranger's vocation.

He decided, "I'll hold on to this till we're almost there, just in case I freak her out." Two hours is an eternity if it starts with an awkward moment. But the prompting got stronger, as if God was relentlessly tapping Simon on the shoulder. Eventually, Simon thought, *Okay, come what may, I've got to share this.*

"Excuse me, ma'am? I know this may sound strange, but I

believe God speaks today, and I feel that God spoke to me about your vocation. Would you mind if I shared?"

"Uh, sure. Yeah, go ahead," she responded, sounding reluctant but intrigued.

He went on to share the word and asked, "Does that resonate with you at all?"

"No, it doesn't," she said. "As a matter of fact, I don't even work in that industry."

"Oh. Uh, okay. Nice to meet you," Simon awkwardly stammered.

That is what learning the Shepherd's voice is like—by risk and obedience. There is no formula for this, only familiarity. We learn God's voice by risk, so we must be willing to get it wrong if we're ever going to get it right. As you take risks, the voice of God becomes more frequent and familiar. And on the flip side, if you're not open to appearing foolish from time to time, you're gonna have a hard time following Jesus and learning the Shepherd's voice.

Prophecy reveals Jesus.

Pastor and author David Fritch writes, "The primary role of the prophetic anointing is to reveal God to the human heart."[10] All prophecy directs us toward Jesus. Old Testament prophecy leads us *to* Jesus. New Testament prophecy leads us along *with* Jesus, the ultimate, embodied revelation of God's heart. In this way, the spiritual gifts of teaching and prophecy are closely related. Teaching is God using a human voice to *tell people about* his character. Prophecy is God using a human voice to *show people* his character.

Some confuse biblical prophecy with future-telling or divinely informed prediction, and occasionally Scripture, particularly in the Old Testament, does have examples of this. But that is not the primary function of the prophetic. "Prophecy does not mean, in the first instance, 'to predict,'" writes author and priest Thomas Green, "but rather to speak on behalf of another."[11] When we understand prophecy as prediction, we are focusing on a peripheral feature of the prophetic, not its primary focus.

It's one thing to be told God loves you. Jesus did that. Through prophecy (among other means), the Holy Spirit pushes the teachings of Jesus from the head, where they can be remembered, down into the heart, where they can heal and become a new foundation for us to live from. Prophecy personally reveals who God is in a way that plunges through the intellect right down to a revelation in the heart.

During the final group gathering at a church retreat I was leading, a friend of mine stood and said, "I have this sense I feel is from the Lord, that there's someone in this room who has a suicide note sitting on their desk at home. You wrote it before you left, and this retreat was your last-ditch effort. You're leaving unsatisfied, and you're planning to take your life when you get home today. I believe God is saying to you, 'I see you. I've heard you. I'm meeting you now. I want you to live.'"

A hush fell over the room. "If that's you, will you just put up your hand?" he went on. "We want to pray for you. As your family, we want to come around you and say, 'Life is worth living, there's a God who's madly in love with you, and there's a community that wants you here.'"

A guy popped up his hand. He had a suicide note on his desk at home, this retreat was a last-ditch effort, he was leaving unsatisfied, and he woke up that morning with every intention of taking his own life before dinner that night. Today, that young man is alive.

It's one thing to be told that Jesus weeps as you weep, that he can empathize with your weakness, that he enters into your pain. That's comforting. It's quite another to discover he saw you and wept beside you while you crafted a note explaining why your life wasn't worth living—and to be told in the most direct way possible that God has numbered your days, they're not up yet, and this isn't the end of your story. That is the power of prophecy—Jesus as generally revealed on the pages of Scripture is personally revealed to me in the midst of today's circumstances.

Prophecy should be eagerly desired by all believers.

Remember Paul's words to the Corinthians: "Follow the way of love and *eagerly desire* gifts of the Spirit, especially prophecy."[12] I don't know about you, but when I eagerly desire something, I think of it constantly, look for every sign of its arrival, and delight in even the small bits of it I get. Every year during the lingering winter months, I eagerly desire the arrival of spring. I look for every bud on every tree and check the weather app constantly for a rise in the temperature. I soak up a sixty-degree day like it's eighty-five.

The English word "eagerly" in this verse is translating the Greek *zeloo*, which literally means "to 'covet' or 'burn with zeal' for a person or a thing."[13] And it's a term Paul uses three times in 1 Corinthians "to describe the attitude we should have toward spiritual gifts."[14]

Some people relate to God's voice passively: "If God wants to speak to me, I'm right here." Behind that posture is often a fear of manufacturing an experience that's less than authentic, and I empathize with that 100 percent. I don't want emotion or hype or to perform psychological tricks on my own mind. But to relate to God's voice passively is also to completely ignore the straightforward teaching of Scripture. We should think constantly about God's still, small whisper. Look for every inkling that he's speaking to us. Soak up every word from his lips like it's the first day of spring. Eager desire is the opposite of passivity.

We in today's church eagerly desire great teaching, and I'm all for that. I love a good sermon. But nowhere in Scripture do we read, "eagerly desire the gift of teaching." The modern focus on teaching is based on the misconception that the words taught or preached to the congregation are the most important words spoken in the worship gathering. God doesn't see it like that. God eagerly desires to pass redemption through one ordinary human vessel to another, so we should eagerly desire to hear his voice.

God doesn't want a team with a few star players. He wants everyone to play. If we really believed that, we'd eagerly desire prophecy. If we really grasped that God is generous and abundant, tenacious in His pursuit of people but equally stubborn and insistent on bringing that redemption through the likes of us, maybe instead of telling God, "I'm here if you want to say anything," we'd ask, "God, what are you saying today? Is there something you want to say to someone else through me?"

PROPHECY IN PRACTICE

The biggest barrier for the modern believer when it comes to prophecy is some version of, "Well, how do I know that's God and not just my imagination?" A good—and important—question. But to address the question, we must first correct the false dichotomy within the question.

In the play *Saint Joan*, there's a scene that's both funny and insightful. Joan of Arc insists that she hears the voice of God. A skeptic says, "That's just your imagination." She responds, "I know. That's how God speaks to me."[15]

Psychologists point to the capacity for imagination as something that distinguishes humans from animals. Only humans can empathize with someone without having shared the same experience, and we do that via the imagination. We can weep with a friend who loses her mother or suffers a miscarriage even if we haven't experienced those things, because we can *imagine* the pain the other person is feeling.

If God uniquely gifted humans with imagination, isn't it a bit backwards to assume that imagination is a hindrance to hearing God's voice? Isn't it more likely that imagination is an important medium for hearing God's voice?

What if you begin to entertain the idea that your imagination—the thoughts that pop into your head involuntarily, the empathy you feel, even the out-of-the-blue idea that seems at first like a distraction—just might be God? I'm not saying that every thought you have is God's voice. But I am saying that God's voice can arrive in cooperation, not competition, with your imagination.

Most people miss the voice of God not because it's too strange but because it's too familiar. I've heard it said that God's voice is like the touch of a feather on your skin, meaning it's light enough that you can ignore it if you want but just clear enough that you can engage and respond if you choose. Pressed to describe hearing God speak, I'd say, "It feels like a thought entering your imagination from the outside, rather than from the inside. It's a normal thought, like any other, but it originates somewhere slightly unfamiliar."

The practice of prophetic prayer involves three major movements: listening, speaking, and receiving.

Listening

As you learn to listen for God's voice, it's important to know that there are three aspects to every prophetic utterance: revelation, interpretation, and application.

Revelation refers to the thought, image, or insight delivered to the listener by the Holy Spirit. In the blank space of waiting after asking God to speak, pay attention to what comes into your imagination—any thoughts that seem to come from without rather than from within. Chances are it'll be something you hear (a word, phrase, or Scripture) or see (a picture, symbol, or memory).

Read the Old Testament prophets and notice how consistently God speaks through images. Isaiah's hot coal, Jeremiah's almond branch, Daniel's ram and goat, or Yahweh's consistent question to Ezekiel, "Son of man, do you see this?" Pictures, images, and symbols—that's God's MO.

Why pictures? If you've got something to say, why not just

come right out and say it? There are lots of reasons, but the most obvious is that a picture is worth a thousand words. You can say a lot more through a picture than in a sentence.

Interpretation is the process of deciphering divine intent and meaning from revelation. When you hear a word or see a picture, the next step is to ask, "Lord, what are you saying through this word or picture?"

Application is the final step. After receiving a revelation and deciphering the interpretation, ask, "What should I do with it?" Is this prophetic insight meant to be shared with an individual, offered to a community or group, prayed into being without sharing aloud, or something else?

It's possible—quite common actually—to get just part of it right. For instance, you may get a word from God, interpret what it means, but misapply it. So there's wisdom in delivering a prophetic word with humility. Avoid absolute language like, "God told me that . . ." Instead, use humble language like, "My sense is that God might want to say . . ."

As it says in 1 Corinthians 13, "We know in part and we prophesy in part."[16] There is no prophet so mature in the gift they don't sometimes miss.

Speaking

As we've already established, God's voice can work in cooperation, not competition, with your imagination. But the question still stands: "How do I know that it's God speaking?"

Pete Greig, in his book *How to Hear God*, says that before you share an impression from God with someone, run it through the ABCs: It should be affirming, biblical, and Christlike.[17]

Affirming. "The one who prophesies speaks to people for their strengthening, encouraging and comfort."[18] If the word isn't affirming, it's probably best to keep it to yourself (more on that below).

Biblical. God speaks through the written Word (Scripture) and the whisper (the still, small voice of the Spirit), but God does not contradict himself. If it doesn't align with Scripture, it's not God speaking and it's not prophecy.

Christlike. Could you imagine Jesus saying it? If it's out of alignment with what you know about the character of Jesus, it's not prophecy.

This filter isn't perfect. There are times when God asks us to speak words of conviction, warning, or disruption rather than affirmation. But those are the exception, and they should be handled by only the most mature, rooted prophets. While Old Testament prophetic expression was quite often rebuke, the New Testament expression—common to all believers for the strengthening of the Body—is directed toward strengthening, encouraging, and comfort. Of course, there are still examples in the New Testament of prophetic words of warning or rebuke. But based on the thematic revelation of the prophetic gift post-Pentecost, it certainly seems like prophecies aimed at rebuke were the minority. Further, prophetic rebuke in the New Testament consistently came through known, respected, seasoned prophets within their local churches.

When you're learning, it's safe to assume God will entrust you with what you can handle. He's a good Father, so if you're just learning to use a pair of scissors, he's unlikely to put a scalpel in your hand and ask you to perform surgery on one of his other children.

Most importantly, when speaking a word of prophecy, do so in love and only in love. Apart from love even the most revelatory prophetic word is nothing but a noisy gong and clanging cymbal.[19] So if you think you have a word for someone but, for whatever reason, can't in good conscience offer it lovingly, give the word back to God and pray for love.[20]

Receiving

Scripture offers instruction both to the one delivering and the one receiving the prophetic word. This is the most frequently overlooked aspect of prophetic ministry and one of the biggest drivers of critiques and fears around this gift.

For the recipient, prophecy should be received freely but weighed carefully. A discerning ear is complementary to a prophetic voice.

Does the word align with the Bible? Does it align with the character of Jesus? There's a lot of warning about watching out for false prophets in the Bible.

Do you trust the character of the prophetic voice? A good life bears good fruit. Does this prophetic word emerge from a fruitful, trustworthy character?

Those who fear the prophetic speak often about the dangers of manipulative prophetic voices. "What are we gonna do about the abuse of the prophetic?" Scripture counsels us exactly what to do: Weigh the word with discernment.

This is one of many key differences in the function of the prophetic gift in the Old and New Testaments. New Testament prophets are not given nearly as much authority as prophets in the Old Testament. The prophet in the church is called to submit the word to the recipient, who has equal access to God's voice and can, therefore, weigh the word given. Prior to Pentecost, prophets were regarded as authoritative voices.

A second difference is that instruction on New Testament prophecy is given to local churches, meaning the function of the prophetic gift is primarily within communities of people who know each other, love each other, and submit together to healthy structures of spiritual authority, leadership, and order: "Two or three prophets should speak, and the others should weigh carefully what is said."[21] Likewise, 1 Thessalonians says to test all prophecies, keeping the good and throwing out the bad.

Scripture never instructs us to silence or avoid the gift of prophecy because we fear it will be abused. Instead, Scripture teaches that prophecy surrenders to love (that's for the speaker), and we honor the gift by weighing the word (that's for the recipient).

Be patient with prophecy. Sometimes a word is trustworthy but doesn't immediately resonate or seem applicable. Every time

I hear a prophetic word about my future (such as "I believe you're coming into a season of joy" or "God is preparing you to be resilient in an upcoming trial") I pray a simple prayer: "God, remind me of this when I need it." From there I put it on the back burner and carry on with my life.

I once received a text message from Maribel, a friend in my community, referencing the words of 1 Peter: "Dear friends, do not be surprised at the fiery ordeal that has come on you." This passage proceeds to claim that there is a way to suffer that produces glory. Maribel said that, when praying for me, this passage had screamed to mind with a sense that I would soon undergo a season of severe trial that would ultimately produce life.

At the time I received the message, it didn't resonate with me in the slightest—just well-intentioned prayer that missed the mark. A week later, though, I found myself in the oncologist's office being informed of a cancerous spread in my body resulting in multiple tumors at the most advanced stage. In the days that followed I clung to this passage for hope, committing it to memory and repeating it in prayer. All that from a friend who prayed for me by listening before speaking.

There have been a few occasions like that, when I was prayerfully reminded of a prophetic word weeks, months, or years later, serving as direction or confirmation at a key moment in my life. There are plenty of other words I've received that haven't come to pass. They're on the back burner, and I'm confident God will remind me of them when and if I need them.

THE POWER OF THE PROPHETIC

Several years ago, Pete Hughes, one of my closest and most trusted friends, came to preach at the church I was leading at the time in Brooklyn. As he closed in prayer, he said, "I've got this nagging thought, and it just might be God so I'm going for it. I think there's someone in the room who's very self-conscious about their teeth. It affects you all the time—guarding your smile, trying not to laugh. You never let your guard down, never stop thinking about it. And I believe God wants to show his love to you today by healing that self-consciousness."

Earlier that morning, Pete had preached at our sister church on the other side of the city, so he added, "Look, to be totally honest, I said this exact same thing across town this morning, and no one responded. So it might just be something weird I ate before bed last night, but I feel led to offer the same invitation again. If that's you, I think God is trying to meet you today, and I'd love to pray with you."

Sure enough, as soon as Pete finished talking, a guy made a beeline to the front. "I attended the service earlier this morning," he said through tears as Pete laid a hand on his shoulder to pray. "When you shared that word I knew it was for me, but I didn't have the nerve to come to the front. I left church, but just couldn't shake that I was meant to respond. I commuted across town to hear you preach the exact same sermon an hour later, saying, 'Alright God, if he says it again, I'll go up.'"

That's not even the best part. Dana, one of my very closest friends, came up for prayer during the time of response that same Sunday.

Through tears, she said, "Tyler, I was gonna tell you today that I'm done with all this church stuff. I don't know what I really believe anymore. But if that's who God is—mighty enough to create but personal enough to speak to one person about insecurity with their smile—I want to know him."

Dana began voicing that desire to God. Six months later she said, "I think God's finally inviting me to meet him, and it's through prayer." Another year after that, she was heading up a team that opened a house of prayer in the heart of the city.

How did all that happen? Pete's willingness to risk became another man's profound moment of encounter with the love of Jesus.

And just by being in the room while a prophetic word was given *to someone else,* Dana's heart was drawn out and her faith restored.

That is the power of prophecy. It reveals Jesus coming after you everywhere you wander, ready to untangle every doubt you've battled, every insecurity you've struggled with, and every lie you've believed.

PRACTICE: ASK & ENCOURAGE

ASK

The gifts of the Spirit are not techniques. They're gifts. A gift isn't something you master—it's something you receive. So if you want an increase in the gift of prophecy, ask God for it in prayer.

And be specific. Tell God not only *what* but also *why* and *how.* Why do you want an increase in the gift of prophecy? How will you use it when he gives it to you? When we ask specifically, our eager desire is refined by the way of love. Our motives get picked apart. Our ego gets weeded out. We are made into mature recipients to use the power of the Spirit's gifts.

Prophecy is a gift for the building up of the church because prophecy surrenders to love. But it's dangerous when it's done from any motive less than selfless love. The prophetic is not about saying what you want to say behind a spiritual disguise, nor is it about making the church into your spiritual playground. Ask and ask specifically so that God can refine your desire by love, entrusting powerful gifts to mature vessels.

ENCOURAGEMENT

One of the ways we grow in prophecy is by fostering the closely related spiritual practice of encouragement. Prophecy involves speaking about things beyond our normal awareness or ability to observe by the Spirit's revelation, while encouragement is based on information available to us through normal observation. In other words, encouragement is prophecy by what *you can see*, and prophecy is encouragement by what *only God can see*.

To encourage literally means "to put courage into someone." It is to notice someone's action, then put the courage in them to keep acting that way and boldly expressing that part of their self: "When you did _____, it looked a lot like redemption. Keep doing your part in redemption."

When you encourage someone, you're not just being nice; you're being like God. You're acting in harmony with his Spirit. How often do you use your words for that purpose?

So if you want to grow in prophecy, start with your eyes open. What have you admired in someone else but never said to their face? Encourage them. What encouraging thought has passed through your mind but never made its way to your lips? Say it.

If you desire prophecy, make a commitment to become a person of encouragement.

NINE

HEALING

Jesus said to her, "I am the resurrection and the life. The one
who believes in me will live, even though they die; and whoever
lives by believing in me will never die. Do you believe this?"

JOHN 11:25–26

"I WAS BENT OVER THE BATHROOM SINK, spitting out some
kind of gunky pus," Tim explained, grimacing at his own description.

It was the culmination of a story that began a week prior.

Tim and his family were on vacation in the San Juan islands, a
remote oasis just off the Seattle coastline. The entire trip, though,
Tim had dealt with the most severe sore throat of his life, growing
worse by the day. By the time they rode the ferry back to the
mainland, he could barely swallow and had eaten very little over
the last two days.

Tim immediately went to the doctor, where he was diagnosed
with a peritonsillar abscess, a growing sore protruding from the
back of his throat that made it nearly impossible to eat or do much
of anything else. Surgery was the only option. Tim scheduled it
for the following day.

Brian, a mutual friend, got caught up on Tim's diagnosis and invited himself over to pray for healing. It was nothing particularly dramatic or eventful. They sat together in the living room as Brian, a bit awkwardly, laid his hand on Tim's neck and prayed in the name of Jesus for the miraculous removal of the abscess and restoration of his throat to its created design.

Nothing happened.

The following morning, Tim passed the hours until surgery playing with his children. It was about fifteen minutes until they needed to walk out the door en route to the hospital. Tim was on the living room floor building something out of Legos with the boys when his mouth suddenly filled with a warm, sour, gunky kind of pus.

When he looked up from the bathroom sink, for the first time in more than a week he was breathing normally, swallowing painlessly, speaking effortlessly.

Tim went on to the hospital, but when the surgeon examined him, there was no longer any need for the operation. The abscess had burst. Tim's body had healed itself. Good as new.

SIGN & SUBSTANCE

The raising of Lazarus is likely Jesus' most astounding miraculous sign outside of his own resurrection. Healing doesn't get more supernatural than raising the dead. But this healing account, maybe more than others, holds the healing ministry of Jesus (a sign of the Kingdom) in proper context next to the salvation offered in Jesus (the substance of the Kingdom).

"Lazarus, come out," Jesus called from the mouth of the tomb. A command that restored life to the dead body of Lazarus, who emerged in his graveclothes. Jesus called out in a loud voice. That's how he raised Lazarus, according to John 11. Surely the disciples were reminded of what he said previously, in John 5: "Very truly I tell you, a time is coming and has now come when the dead will hear the voice of the Son of God and those who hear will live . . . *Do not be amazed at this*, for a time is coming when all who are in their graves will hear his voice and come out—those who have done what is good will rise to live, and those who have done what is evil will rise to be condemned."[1]

In the resurrection of Lazarus, Jesus was reaching back to a promise he made in John 5, but he's also reaching forward to his own resurrection in John 20. The sign is a miracle pointing to a person: Jesus. The miraculous intervention of God is a sign—a real, tangible, supernatural reality—that points to a promise. But the sign is not the promise itself. *Healing is a sign of the Kingdom that points to salvation, the substance of the Kingdom.*

Jesus says to the grieving, "I am the resurrection and the life." Then he calls Lazarus out of the grave. There's hope now! Not an abstract, far-off, sentimental hope but real, embodied hope here and now in our midst! *That's the sign.*

Then Jesus suffers, dies, is put in his own tomb, and walks out three days later. There's hope forever—hope that will never be taken away. *That's the substance.*

HEALING: A SIGN

Genesis starts with the creation of embodied humanity—made in God's image and called "good." Sin interrupts that goodness, and the effects of sin get into every aspect of creation—thoughts, choices, relationships, systems, and our bodies. With sin came sickness, disease, and death. Creation came with an embodied blessing from God and sin came with an embodied curse.

God dealt with that curse by taking on a body. In his resurrection, Jesus' body conquered all of sin's consequences, including sickness, suffering, and death. The final victory is still future, but the promise is already here: We will be raised with Christ—and raised bodily. Heaven, according to Jesus and the biblical authors, is not an escape. It's a renewal—the renewal of the earth and the renewal of our bodies.

The healing of the body, then, is a sign: a preview of the promised future, an aspect of the inbreaking Kingdom of God we know now in part but one day will know fully.

Healing is biblical.

Supernatural, miraculous healing is all over the Bible.

Genesis 20 records that Abraham prayed for Abimelech and his wife, who were infertile, and they were healed and had children. Elijah raised a boy from the dead in 1 Kings 17. In 2 Kings 5, Elisha healed Naaman of leprosy.

In the Gospels, Jesus opened the eyes of the blind, cleansed lepers, stopped the bleeding of a hemorrhaging woman, stood up a paralytic or two, and called Lazarus out of his tomb.

Peter and John healed a lame beggar at the temple in Acts 3. In Acts 5, we're told healing was so common that people were trying to catch Peter's shadow when he walked by in case it had healing power. In Acts 20, Paul brought to life someone who had fallen to their death from a third-story window ledge.

Healing is a part of the church's ministry.

Four of the five times Jesus told his disciples to declare the message of the Kingdom, he commanded them to heal the sick in the same breath. The supernatural healing of the body was a relatively common occurrence in the book of Acts, and it's listed as one of the gifts of the Spirit given to the church in 1 Corinthians.

The Bible neither shies away from nor sensationalizes healing. Healing is not extra special, nor is it hush-hush. It's just another ministry of the church—like preaching, wisdom, encouragement, administration, and prophecy.

Healing is complicated.

Healing is complicated because suffering is real and suffering hurts. Healing is most often sought in the midst of suffering, so when we seek healing we're asking God to touch something that's probably already life-defining and make it life-redefining. Whether God brings healing or not, our stories of experiencing illness and seeking healing are sure to change us forever.

This is the one aspect that, I believe, distinguishes healing from other spiritual gifts. Many people—not all, but many—respond to bad teaching with a yawn. But many people respond to an unmet request for healing by redefining the God they pray to. Some holding this book have a story of healing. Others have a story of suffering. And plenty of us have both.

We live in a tension theologians call the "already/not yet." Jesus has been victorious over sin, and we can know that victory here and now—"Already." But the full experience of that victory is still future, awaiting Jesus' return—"Not yet." Over a lifetime of apprenticeship to Jesus, you will experience the overwhelming joy of the "already," and you will experience the pain of the "not yet." That tension is made bearable only by the God who didn't shy away from either—by Jesus who was both a victorious Savior ushering in a Kingdom and a man of sorrows, a suffering servant.

Healing is complicated and requires a community of spiritual maturity and pastoral sensitivity.

Healing is not as complicated as we tend to make it.

Of course, we keep praying for healing despite a less than 100 percent success rate because *healing is a sign of the Kingdom.* When someone preaches a sermon and every lost person doesn't come to faith, we don't begin doubting God wants to seek and save the lost. We don't abandon preaching the gospel. Teaching and healing are both spiritual gifts according to the Bible. Because healing is a spiritual gift, that means we can grow in power when it comes to healing, just like we can grow in teaching, service, prophecy, and the other gifts.

So if you're wondering, "Is it God's will to heal?" yes, of course God wills healing. God will heal all of our embodied pain. That's a promise. What we're unclear on is *when* and *how* healing will occur—in this life or the next, through a miracle now or through our eventual resurrection.

If you're wondering, "Why didn't God heal?" in a particular situation, that's a more complicated question, one without a clean and tidy biblical answer. We'll get into that some more in a minute. But for now, let me say, the safest thing about praying for healing is that the God we pray to is so good that he repurposes everything—*everything*, even our suffering—into our redemption. God can and will redeem everything you experience in this life if you offer it to him.

So yes, healing is complicated, but not as complicated as we tend to make it.

If I had to sum up all of that in a single phrase, I'd probably go with this: *Healing is an "already" taste of the "not yet" eternal life we still await.*

SALVATION: THE SUBSTANCE

Many people, when they hear the word "salvation," think of altar calls and "repeat after me" prayers. I'm not inherently opposed to any of that, but it's not salvation. Biblically, salvation is about what Jesus has done for us, and it's also about what Jesus is doing and will do for us. Salvation is a life, not just a rescue. Salvation includes forgiveness of sins but also goes beyond forgiveness to the redeemed life won by grace. Christian philosopher Dallas Willard explains, "The message of Jesus himself and of the early disciples was not one just of forgiveness of sins, but rather one of newness of life."[2]

Healing is a sign pointing to a Kingdom that's coming. Coming whether you want it or not. Coming whether you see it or not. Coming for sure and coming for good (in both senses of the word "good"—it's for our good *and* it's here to stay). But healing is not the Kingdom itself—it's not life and life to the full and life forever. It's not salvation, not the substance, only a sign. That's why . . .

Healing is often a bridge to salvation.

Healing the body is one way God makes his appeal to a whole person—body, soul, and spirit. It's why often, right alongside an account of miraculous physical healing, Jesus would say something like, "Your sins are forgiven." Salvation is something that we experience in this age and in the age to come—it's for right now and it's forever. On the other hand . . .

All healing this side of heaven is temporary.

Everyone who gets miraculously healed will get sick or injured again. Their body will wear out with age and ultimately die. The blind man Bartimaeus had his eyes opened, but one day death closed those eyes again. The paralytic picked up his mat and walked, but one day he was laid down again in a casket. Lazarus walked out of a tomb, but later he had a second funeral.

It's still true that Jesus has defeated death by his resurrection! And we experience signs of resurrection life here and now through healing. But don't confuse a sign with the substance. Don't confuse a little taste of healing today with the forever feast that's coming.

Jesus was *resurrected*. Death couldn't hold him. Lazarus was just *resuscitated*. He got more days, but death was still his fate. But think about the quality of those days after his resuscitation! The otherwise ordinary days were surely charged with the glory of God. The miraculous glory of the Lord is properly stewarded when it opens our eyes to the everyday glory of the Lord—the sacred quality of this person, this moment.

Practically speaking, all of that means . . .

Every sign should be sought in right Kingdom perspective.

If you get miraculously healed today, you might wake up with a headache tomorrow. Our ultimate hope is not resting on healing today but on resurrection. As the apostle Paul so boldly proclaimed, "If only for this life we have hope in Christ, we are of all people most to be pitied."[3]

Every sign should be eagerly desired and sought with passion and excitement.

My middle son, Simon, has his sixth birthday coming up in just few weeks. I know all kids have a weakness for sweets, but this dude is next level. All he thinks about is cake. If he knows a cake is coming and he's gotta finish his veggies for a slice, he can eat a plate of raw spinach in less than sixty seconds.

And Simon loves to help in the kitchen, but the truth is he's got an ulterior motive. No matter what you're making—pancakes, cookies, or birthday cake—my man always asks for a taste. He's in it for that batter-covered spoon that someone's gonna get to lick off, and he's staying next to the chef to ensure he's the lucky recipient.

Since Simon's birthday is coming, that means at some point I'll be in the kitchen and cake will be on the menu. He knows that when I (his father) am preparing a feast, I have trouble resisting when he asks for a little taste of the celebration early.

That's what healing is. Healing is a taste of the batter when a cake is coming. Our posture toward healing should be like Simon's—childlike, filled with wonder, desperate for a taste, wanting it so bad we can't stand it, ready to trade anything for one lick of that batter-coated spoon. But we also need to be absolutely certain that we've got a whole cake coming, absolutely certain that this taste isn't the best thing or the whole thing. This taste is just a preview of what's promised.

Healing is not the Kingdom, so it's not where our ultimate hope lies. But it is a sign of the Kingdom, so we seek it and ask for it now, hungry for a taste of what's to come.

How do I pray for healing?

Author Jordan Seng points out that while Jesus healed frequently in the Gospels, he left a lot to be desired for those in search of a model:

> One of the fascinating things about studying healing ministry in Scripture is the wonderfully diverse way the many stories of healing unfold. Peter's mother-in-law was healed as soon as Jesus took her hand, but the ten lepers didn't experience their healing until after Jesus had sent them away. Jesus healed a servant's ear by touching it, but the hemorrhaging woman was healed when she sneaked up on Jesus and touched him. Jairus's daughter was resurrected from death immediately when Jesus called her, but the blind man in Bethsaida needed Jesus to touch him twice before he saw clearly. Jesus ordered a man to stretch out his withered hand, and the man was healed as he tried the impossible, but the centurion's servant was healed over a considerable distance just by Jesus' word. The paralytic lowered down to Jesus through a roof was first forgiven of his sins and then healed, but when Jesus healed the man born blind, he assured his disciples that sin played no part in the affliction. Jesus first delivered the hunched-back woman from a demonic spirit of infirmity and then touched her spine to heal it, but the Canaanite girl wasn't even present when Jesus delivered and healed her through a proclamation to her mother. Jesus distributed healings through touch, commands, and declarations. Sometimes he applied saliva, sometimes mud. Sometimes just touching his cloak was enough.[4]

If you're looking for a step-by-step approach to supernatural healing, the Bible just isn't your book. There's mystery to the miraculous. But we can get *some* clarity by looking at examples of those who have put healing prayer into practice.

HANK'S SHOULDER

We had two flights of stairs leading to our Brooklyn apartment. Our son Hank, two years old at the time, always wanted to be carried up, but we were trying to teach him to walk the stairs. Each time we entered the building, little Hank would flop down in front of the first step, waiting until we broke down and carried him up.

On this particular Friday evening, when Hank began his usual protest, I drew a clear line in the sand. I told him no—an easy word to speak but a hard word for a two-year-old to hear. Taking hold of his left hand in my right, we began the ascent.

Children who are tired occasionally allow their bodies to fall limp. Losing the will to go on, they will suddenly drop their full weight anywhere at any given moment. Hank enacted that routine somewhere near the top step. His hand was in mine, and when he dropped his weight this time, he screamed—screamed like I've never heard him scream before.

Immediately when we walked into the apartment, I tried to get him to throw me a ball, but he couldn't even lift his arm. I put a spoonful of ice cream in his left hand, but when he lifted the spoon to his mouth, he only got his hand about chest high before yelping in pain. I determined that his shoulder was likely dislocated. We were soon walking to urgent care in a New York City snowstorm.

Though I'd had no anger in the moment he'd gotten hurt, and I knew objectively I'd done nothing wrong, I also had an indescribably awful feeling in the pit of my stomach. *Will he remember this? Will this be his first memory of me? Will this affect him long term? Will they have me questioned by the police at urgent care for possible abuse?*

The attending pediatrician confirmed our suspicions after an X-ray. Hank's rotator cuff wasn't torn. No ligament damage. But his shoulder was dislocated. And given how malleable a toddler's bones are, not just any doctor could be trusted with the art of putting his arm back where God put it first. The soonest we could see a pediatric orthopedist would be the following morning at a pediatric ER.

That night was one of the worst of my life. Hank woke up countless times. Every time he rolled onto that shoulder, pain radiated down his arm and through his chest. Startled awake repeatedly by the sting, Hank wailed in his crib and hardly slept. I'm not sure I slept at all.

The following morning, just before we walked out the door, a thought occurred to Kirsten: "We should invite Simon over to pray for Hank before we go." Simon was one of the elders at our church, a man particularly full of faith for supernatural healing. He was out when we called. Risking an escalating wait time on what was already guaranteed to be a tumultuous Saturday, Kirsten felt convicted we should wait, that we should pray for a miracle before leaving home.

Simon arrived an hour later. He walked in with anointing oil, following the instructions for the healing prayer of elders in James chapter 5. We sat together in the living room, Simon and Kirsten on the leather couch, me across from them in a mossy green armchair, and Hank between the three of us on the rug.

Simon prayed that ancient prayer, "Come, Holy Spirit," and waited in silence. That silence was broken about twenty seconds later when Kirsten prayed matter-of-factly, "God, I know you *can* heal, but I don't think you *will*. I would happily stand in front of a church and theoretically explain that I believe in a healing God, but I can't honestly pray for my own son with any faith you'll actually do something about his pain. To be completely honest, I don't think you care about this. I think you might heal malnutrition in an impoverished child or leukemia in someone on their death bed, but I don't think you care about little Hank's shoulder. I repent. I repent of my unbelief. Help me with my doubt."

As Kirsten was contritely divulging all of that to God, I sat with my eyes open, fixed on the ground. I saw Hank moving out of the corner of my eye and looked up. Hank picked up his favorite book, held it in his left hand, and reached up, offering the book to me. He extended his arm well above his head, asking me to read it to him. Surprised and curious, I placed a ball that was sitting at my feet in his left hand. Immediately, he rifled it back to me. Emboldened, I gently picked him up by his two hands, pulling his full weight up by his arms. He laughed, thinking I was playing with him.

"Guys, look!" I exclaimed.

Hank's dislocated shoulder was completely restored in an instant. I've never seen anything like it. "It worked!" I gasped. "I can't believe it! It worked!"

20/20 VISION

My friend Pete Portal oversees Tree of Life, a beautiful community working to rehabilitate addicts and gang members in Manenberg, South Africa. Recently, at their community's monthly worship night, something extraordinary happened. A couple different people came forward with dramatic stories of how they'd come in quite skeptical, but God had healed them of some physical pain or sickness that very evening. Now, as the evening was drawing to a close, the skeptics were in tears praising Jesus as healer.

But here's the really fun part: The man running slides at the back wore glasses for nearsightedness. He was sitting in the booth tracking through the lyrics, and suddenly he couldn't see the screen clearly. In an instant everything had gone blurry and out of focus. He slipped off his glasses, and to his amazement, he could see perfectly.

He later shared that at the beginning of the night, he'd muttered a short prayer from behind the booth, asking God to give him some obvious sign that this whole worship experience was really about God and not just well-meaning well-wishers talking themselves into a group-think variety of belief. And now, as the band played the final song, he could see with 20/20 vision!

BROOKS'S HEART

After a brutal period of two open-heart surgeries in just five years, it seemed this straw would finally break the camel's back. Brooks was, yet again, putting his life in the hands of surgeons as they attempted for the third time to repair his failing heart. "He needs immediate surgery. High likelihood of death regardless, but we gotta give this a try. It's his only shot."

Brooks's health insurance was a nightmare, leading to delays in scheduling a surgery, which can be particularly anxiety inducing when your life's on the clock as it is. In the meantime, plenty of people wanted to pray for Brooks, and he let them go for it. Why not? What did he have to lose?

It was more than just "why not?" though. Brooks actually had a conviction that God wanted to physically heal him. This was no naive conviction or misguided demand for divine healing, either. Just a humble hunch forged in prayer that somehow this pain in his body would be repurposed as a spectacle of God's glory—and that was a hunch he had not felt for the previous two heart surgeries.

Ultra-charismatic faith-healer types were revolving through Brooks's home praying their best, most sincere prayers. Nothing was happening—nothing visible at least—and the days kept ticking by.

The week of the scheduled surgery arrived, and because of the pessimistic prognosis, Brooks was instructed to live like this was his last week. On what might be his last Sunday, Brooks went to church with his parents. He usually attended a church in a different part of town, but on this particular day with so much to process, he preferred a community among whom he could worship in complete anonymity.

During the opening worship song, a young stranger, not a day over twenty-five, approached and said, "Hey, you're Brooks, right?"

"Yeah, that's me."

"Great!" The young stranger seemed unnervingly enthusiastic about the connection. "There's this guy in our church who's been really wanting to press into healing prayer. You mind coming with me? I know your story. He could pray for you."

So much for anonymity, but Brooks is never one to turn down prayer.

The young guy led Brooks to the front row, where he tapped this gentleman on the shoulder and explained, "Hey, you've been thinking a lot about healing prayer. Brooks has a horrific diagnosis and needs a miracle. What do you think?"

This man looked like a deer in the headlights. It was at this point that Brooks realized he was not the only one caught up in an unexpected experience. This man laid his hand on Brooks's chest and began to pray. The two of them looked like an odd pair: complete strangers yet interacting so intimately. Two people who didn't have a single thing in common but Jesus, with one asking for God to intervene miraculously in the desperate need of the other.

The prayer that followed was nothing special—short, simple, to the point. It wasn't particularly eloquent or lengthy and sounded more conversational than lyrical. "But as he prayed I felt this incredible heat on my chest," Brooks remembered. "It was almost unbearable, like my chest was on fire. When he said, 'Amen,' I walked back to my seat wondering, 'Did you just heal me, God?'"

The following week Brooks was scheduled for a final set of pre-op chest scans. Three days after those scans, Brooks got a call from his doctor.

"I have extraordinary news. You have no infection. We must've misdiagnosed you to begin with," the doctor explained.

"No, you didn't get it wrong. Look at my previous scans!" Brooks responded.

"I'm looking at them now. I see the infection on those scans," the doctor said. And getting ahead of the assumed follow-up question, he added, "And no, there's no infection on the new scans. I don't know how to explain it."

As Brooks relayed the story to me through tears and laughter, still buzzing with the miraculous spectacle of it all, he said of the prayer that instigated his healing, "Of course you'd do it that way, God. Of course you'd bypass the prayers of all those experienced faith-healer people, waiting to honor the simple prayer of a sincere guy who seemed to have little miraculous experience but plenty of humble hunger and active faith for what he was yet to experience."

———

So how does healing happen? Well, for Hank, my wife's repentance did the trick. And for that volunteer running the slides it took a personal prayer, whispered in the back, that no one ever heard. And for Brooks it happened by a single prayer with the laying on of hands.

There is no formula.

So why did those healings happen?

Because of expertise in the methods of healing prayer? No. The man who prayed for Brooks had no experience in healing ministry and had never seen someone healed through prayer, much less been the conduit.

Because of a particularly devout faith on the part of those praying or receiving healing? No. Kirsten prayed her doubt, and in Pete's community, three people on the receiving end of God's healing power admitted they'd started the evening full of skepticism.

Why, then? Why did those healings happen and not others?

I don't know. That's the only honest response.

What I definitely *do* know is that if you prayed for a person only to watch them suffer, it's not because you didn't have the right words, the right faith, or the right technique. Healing isn't a magic trick, awaiting a magician who knows the spell. It's one of the ways God shows us his love. Priest and spiritual director Albert Haase simply writes: "Healing is not an achievement; it is a gift."[5]

If you read the Bible to discover *if* God wants to heal today, you get a clear, straightforward answer: yes. If you read the Bible to discover *how* to join God in healing, you leave more confused than you came. There's mystery to the miraculous. Scripture doesn't provide a formula. Neither does Scripture keep us entirely in the dark, though.

Healing is a batter-coated spoon when a cake is coming, remember? And just as Simon doesn't know the recipe to bake a cake, neither do I know the recipe to divine healing. Like Simon, though, if you linger around the kitchen often enough, you learn the ingredients, even if you're still clueless on the measurements and instructions. Scripture does offer us that much, and we'll explore the ingredients to healing prayer when we get to this chapter's practice.

NEPHESH

A few months after the miraculous, gunky pus incident, Tim reflected on the experience and, with the help of others, began to connect the dots. Tim's healing had come at the end of a profound year of spiritual renewal, in which God had been healing his soul and breathing fresh spiritual life into him in a number of ways.

In addition to being a friend and participant in our church

here in Portland, Tim Mackie is one of the main voices of *The Bible Project*, a globally renowned ministry that helps people experience the Bible as a unified story that leads to Jesus. Within their catalogue of resources, Tim has done a lot of work on the Hebrew word *nephesh*, which appears over seven hundred times in the Old Testament. The common English translation of this word is "soul," but, interestingly, it most literally means "throat."

The English word "soul" is most broadly imagined as the nonphysical essence of a person separated from the body at death. That understanding has its roots in the later Greek understanding. The biblical understanding of the soul is quite different, though. While *nephesh* most literally means "throat," ancient Israelites used it to refer to the whole person, since what passes in and out of one's throat nourishes and expresses the whole life and body. In the Bible, people don't have a *nephesh*, which is separated from the body at death. People *are* a *nephesh*: a living, breathing, spiritual being.

"You do see the substance this sign points to, don't you?" a friend asked Tim. "He wasn't just healing your throat," she continued. "He was healing your *nephesh*. God has been healing your whole person and promises to go on healing you until you're completely whole and fully alive."

Tim's eyes widened. He began to see that the healing of his throat was more than just the removal of his bodily suffering, the bypassing of medical bills, or a fun story to tell. It was a sign of the Kingdom, an "already" taste of the "not yet" eternal life we still await.

Tim's healing was an embodied way God was speaking his greatest, broadest, and most personal promise in a language Tim could understand and receive deeply and personally. And that's what the Holy Spirit does: translate the sure promises of Jesus into physical, tangible experiences on which we build our hope as we await the fullness of our salvation.

PRACTICE: THE SIX INGREDIENTS OF HEALING PRAYER

1. FAITH IS A FACTOR

In Mark 6, in the throes of his growing miraculous ministry, Jesus returned to his hometown. We read, "He could not do any miracles there, except lay his hands on a few sick people and heal them. He was amazed *at their lack of faith*."[6]

A few chapters later, we see the other side of the same coin when Jesus heals the blind man Bartimaeus. "'Go,' said Jesus, *'your faith has healed you*.' Immediately he received his sight."[7]

The Bible clearly presents faith as a key ingredient to healing.

As a quick word of caution, though, shame or condemnation can come along with acknowledging this truth. Some may think, *God would've healed that person, but I didn't have enough faith.* That's absolutely not what I'm saying. Faith is one of the ingredients to healing yet there are other factors, and there's a lot of mystery.

But I can say this with confidence: God wants to heal. Faith plays a part in healing. And God is merciful and gracious, slow to anger, and abounding in steadfast love,[8] so if you feel shame or condemnation, that's not God condemning you; it's the deceiver. Throw it out.

2. PREPARATION MATTERS

Mark 9 tells the story of Jesus healing a boy suffering from epilepsy, a disease that was, in this instance, demonic in its origin. Jesus rolled up on the disciples, who had been unable to heal the boy, and said something interesting: "This kind only comes out by prayer and fasting."[9] Prayer and fasting is shorthand language for consecration, a term meaning "to set aside as holy." Prayer and fasting are ways we set our lives aside as holy and make ourselves available for sacred use.

When you give more of your life to God, you grow in spiritual power. If you want the gift of healing, give more of yourself to prayer and fasting. "It isn't about having ministers who know how to pray for the sick," writes Jordan Seng. "It's about having ministers who are steeped in the obedience, faith, gifting, and consecration that lead to spiritual power."[10]

3. SIMPLE PRAYER IS ALL IT TAKES

The most underrated teaching Jesus ever gave on prayer is, "And when you pray, do not keep on babbling like pagans, for they think they will be heard because of their many words. Do not be like them."[11]

Here's a survey of the prayers or commands of Jesus resulting in miraculous healing:

- To a leper: "Be clean!"[12]
- To a deceased boy: "Young man, I say to you, get up!"[13]
- To a paralytic: "Get up, take your mat and go home."[14]
- And Peter, in the early days of church history, mimicked his rabbi's approach: "In the name of Jesus Christ of Nazareth, walk."[15]

Each command or prayer is incredibly simple. When we pray long, eloquent prayers asking for the miraculous, we betray our unspoken belief that God's more likely to respond if we rile him up with a great speech.

When it comes to healing prayer, you must remember: God wants this more than you do. No matter who you are or what your story is, no one wants your healing more than the God who is love, so simple prayer will do.

4. PERSISTENCE MAY BE REQUIRED

Persistence features frequently in biblical accounts of healing, including the story in Mark 8 when Jesus spat in the dirt, rubbed it in the eyes of a blind man, and asked, "Can you see now?" The man's vision was improved but not healed. People appeared like blurred trees moving about. So Jesus spat and tried again, finally resulting in complete healing.

When we pray for healing, we may see slight improvement and need to keep praying. If Jesus—someone perfectly in touch with the Spirit's power—had to do that, we should expect the same.

John Wimber left behind a remarkable legacy of supernatural healing that wasn't born from hype or manipulation but from the Spirit's power. When asked how it happened, he said, "We prayed and prayed for healing and we were disappointed and disappointed. We kept at it for nine or ten months, and finally, we got one! Then we prayed twice as much for twice as long until finally, we got another! That's when the floodgates opened, and the healing we sought persistently became ordinary."[16]

5. BOTH HEALING AND SUFFERING ARE REDEMPTIVE

I devote a full chapter to the redemptive power of suffering in the pages to come, so for now I'll keep it simple and straightforward: Jesus was a miraculous healer, but by far his most effective act of healing came by suffering and ultimately dying on a cross. "By his wounds we are healed."[17]

And the Bible, which is peppered cover-to-cover with miraculous healing, is also peppered cover-to-cover with redemptive suffering. Minister and activist Kenneth Leech advises that prayers for physical healing be prayed while holding a cross, a tangible reminder that it's Jesus' wounds that bring our fullest healing.[18]

Jesus has not revealed a God with satisfying answers to our individual stories and questions, but he has provided a God who suffered and suffers alongside us, is personally acquainted with the cost of suffering, and has emphatically promised to never let a drop of my suffering or yours go to waste.

6. HEALING PRAYER NEVER REPLACES MEDICINE

I'd never counsel anyone to pursue supernatural healing *instead of* medical healing. There is no biblical precedent for that, and a well-formed theology of healing includes medical healing. God heals often through medicine and sometimes without it (or beyond its limits). It is a de-formed theology that pits medical healing *against* biblical healing.

There you have it: the biblical ingredients to supernatural healing. But it's not a recipe. Everyone who acquires a taste for the wondrous Kingdom sign of miraculous healing in this life also stomachs plenty of disappointment. We can pray for healing by keeping the sign in proper perspective with the substance and trusting that, while Jesus has not revealed a God we can perfectly understand, he has revealed a God we can perfectly trust.

TEN

WITNESS

But you will receive power when the Holy Spirit comes on you;
and you will be my witnesses in Jerusalem, and in all Judea
and Samaria, and to the ends of the earth.

ACTS 1:8

MELANIE SAT SPEECHLESS after hanging up the phone. Jayla
sounded shaken. No, more than shaken—scared—as she relayed
the news. Her mother had overdosed. Jayla and her siblings had
suddenly become the responsibility of the Department of Child
Services. And in the snap of a finger, all four children, who'd never
spent a night apart in their lives, were separated into different
foster homes. Jayla, the oldest at sixteen, had always carried herself
more like an adult—hardened and tough. But the shock of it all
had reduced her to a child—lost, afraid, and alone.

Months prior to that call, Melanie had met Jayla while volunteering at an inner city mentorship program. In the weeks that
followed, Melanie and her husband, Ray, also got to know Jayla's
mother and three siblings. Guided by the Holy Spirit through
prayer, Melanie and Ray began to serve the family holistically

by meeting practical and financial needs and providing housing assistance. Ray owns a few residential buildings in Nashville, and Jayla's family eventually moved out of government-subsidized housing into one of his condos. They seemed to be thriving. It was all unfolding like a storybook until that phone call when everything changed.

Melanie was stunned. She and Ray had no idea what to do. They were worried for the kids, confused by the process, and wondering who would advocate for these four voiceless children. After looking at Melanie in silence, Ray dropped his head in his hands and began to pray, asking the Holy Spirit for help, for wisdom, for guidance.

That prayer turned out to be a slippery slope of the most redemptive variety. A few months later, Ray and Melanie had become the foster parents to all four kids and were in the grind of the official adoption process. They had not had a void in their life they needed to fill. They had not been in search of meaning or purpose. They hadn't been led by a naive Savior complex. But they were guided by the Holy Spirit's whisper through the noisy desperation of sudden grief and urgent need.

I guess, in a way, you could say that Ray's prayer completely messed up their plans. All this did happen, mind you, to a couple of empty nesters who'd already put in their time parenting and were on to the next chapter. At a stage in life they thought would be about relaxing, slowing down, and taking the weekend escapes they had deferred in the frenzy of middle age, they instead became parents to four rambunctious kids. Many of their friends thought (and think) they're crazy. And who knows? Maybe they are.

But in another way, you could say that prayer saved their lives. It defined their plans according the Spirit's invitation rather than cultural norms. Thomas Merton once said it is dangerous business to ask the Holy Spirit to help you because the Holy Spirit teaches us to die.[1] And Jesus says that dying to self—losing our lives—is the only way to save them. So within the biblical imagination, this "disruption" was yet another invitation to life—the full, free, abundant life promised us in Jesus.

And you know what? Ray and Melanie's choice felt like a death of sorts. As the weeks have turned to years there's been plenty of dysfunction, disagreement, and both generational and cross-cultural learning required. It's been hard every step of the way. Objectively speaking, it's been a whole lot harder than empty nesting as advertised: propping your feet up on the beach-house porch stirring a martini.

At the same time it's been life—a story of adventure that only those who follow Jesus get to inherit, an adventure they'd never trade for some version of the American dream. The guidance of the Holy Spirit landed Ray and Melanie in a plot they never consciously pursued. Because of love: radical, sacrificial, "never would've done it but I took this risk called prayer" sort of love. And costly love has a way of filling the human heart with meaning and life in a way that comfort, indulgence, and days of uninterrupted relaxation can never touch.

Prayer—that's the dangerous place they turned for guidance amid desperation, and the Holy Spirit taught these seasoned saints to die another death. To die that they might come even more alive.

GO, BUT WAIT

Jesus' final appearances to his disciples before his ascension seem to carry a contradictory message: "Go, but wait." He issues words and instructions of sending, most notably in the Great Commission,[2] but he also cautions them to wait for the promised Spirit of power rather than go on their own.

Jesus' final words in Luke's gospel are, "Stay in the city until you have been clothed with power from on high."[3] Luke's second book, Acts, opens with the same sentiment: "Do not leave Jerusalem, but wait for the gift my Father promised."[4]

"Go, but wait." That's the limbo the disciples are left in between the ascension of Jesus in Acts 1 and the gift of the Spirit in Acts 2.

It seems that the risen Messiah is aware that we will forever be tempted to go on our own strength, relying on our own power, rather than being empowered by the Spirit.

"Lord, are you at this time going to restore the kingdom to Israel?"[5] That was the disciples' question. They interrupted Jesus' last words—when he's explaining one final time that his very Spirit is about to plunge into the inner lives of each one of them—to ask *that* question. It's revealing. Even on this side of the cross and empty tomb, the disciples are still imagining a political kingdom built on power and achieved by force. They are still thinking about "kingdom come" in this world's terms when Jesus has been operating from an otherworldly paradigm all along.

Before receiving the Spirit, the disciples were thinking about a triumphant nation. After receiving the Spirit, the disciples are thinking about a new humanity. Their eyes have widened and their imaginations have expanded from all that Jesus won for us through his spotless life, sacrificial death, and triumphant resurrection.

We, like the disciples, are forever susceptible to getting ahead of Jesus. Assuming we know the plot of the story, we rush into action rather than waiting on the Spirit to empower and guide our action. The ministry of Jesus, energized by human willpower rather than the Holy Spirit, always results in pain. We may be well-intentioned, but the renewal of the world requires a greater wisdom than the human imagination and a greater power than human effort.

The Holy Spirit was first experienced in the safe company of the apostles in the enclosed upper room at the culmination of a forty-nine-day prayer meeting. But that same Spirit quickly led those very people beyond the cozy confines of their gathering and into mission. It wasn't their idea to go to the paralyzed beggar on the temple steps and to the hungry widows, but that's where the Spirit drove them. It wasn't their idea to open the Scriptures with Ethiopian eunuchs, worship with Gentiles, and break bread with Samaritans, but that's where the Spirit led them.

Theologian Michael Green writes, "The Comforter comes not in order to allow [people] to be comfortable, but to make them missionaries . . . it is the Spirit who energizes the evangelism of the Church and drives its often unwilling members into the task for which God laid his hand on them: mission."[6]

Some use the term "Spirit-filled" to refer to churches most active in their *gathered* worship—communities enthusiastic in their praise, wild in their worship, and charismatic in their practice. But maybe we've got it backwards? Maybe the "Spirit-filled" community is the one most active in their *scattered* worship? The life of the Holy Spirit sends us *out* in power, commissioning us to live in this world in a way that spreads rumors of another world.

YOU WILL BE MY WITNESSES

Jesus' final instruction before Pentecost was, in summary, "You won't understand the whole story or even the part you're playing in the story with your one, short, wild life, but here's what you can be sure of: The Holy Spirit will give you power and make you *witnesses.*"

Witness literally means "someone who sees or experiences something important for others to know about." Somewhere along the way in recent church history, "witness" became a synonym for "evangelism." And while witness does include telling people the good news about Jesus, that's only part of it. Theologian N. T. Wright says,

Modern Christians use the word "witness" to mean "tell some-one else about your faith." The way Luke seems to be using it is, "tell someone else that Jesus is the world's true Lord." The story of what happened next is written in such a way as to say, "This is how the kingdom is to come. This is how Jesus is starting to rule the world. This is what it will look like when God becomes king on earth as in heaven."[7]

The Kingdom of God was Jesus' way of talking about the rule and order of heaven coming to blanket the earth. Jesus brought God's Kingdom to earth in three ways—teaching, miracles, and sacrifice.

- Jesus' *teaching* paints a picture of full life through divine for-giveness and grace—not human perfection or performance.
- Jesus' *miracles* reveal God's Kingdom will be a time and place where human suffering—sickness, poverty, oppres-sion, natural disaster, and death—will be banished.
- Jesus' *sacrifice* means God's Kingdom will be a time and place of reconciliation—restored union between God and humanity.

The Holy Spirit makes us witnesses of these great truths, meaning the full ministry of Jesus is distributed to every one of Jesus' followers by the third person of the Trinity. The Holy Spirit empowers every one of Jesus' followers to bring his Kingdom on earth as it is in heaven.

Jesus came as the King of a new Kingdom. Witnesses are those who live in this contested world under the reign of Jesus and his coming Kingdom. To bear witness to Jesus takes on an endless array of expressions, like the endless variety of colors in a color wheel. But, just as every shade is traced back to three primary col-ors, we can trace every expression of witness back to three primary expressions—*spoken love*, *supernatural love*, and *sacrificial love*.

SPOKEN LOVE

It's important to acknowledge the tension we live in as Jesus' followers. On one hand, evangelism is terribly out of style. It evokes the image of a street corner bullhorn or "turn or burn" homemade sign. No one likes to be "evangelized to," whether it's about a timeshare in Tahiti, an essential oils pyramid scheme, or Jesus of Nazareth. The most outspoken "evangelists" are often "speaking love" in a way that feels, somehow, highly confrontational and completely unloving. On the other hand, preaching the gospel is a central priority of Jesus. He is the Good Shepherd who leaves the ninety-nine to go after the one. He is the Son of Man who came to seek and save the lost. And he commissioned all his followers to share the message of the gospel. We live in the tension between "out-of-style evangelism" and "the priorities of Jesus."

So maybe I could relieve a little bit of the tension by reminding you that everyone's preaching *a gospel*.

A couple weeks ago, I was standing by the front door of my local gym, awaiting a Lyft ride that was an unthinkable nine minutes away. Two guys were working the front desk together. One of them, based on their conversation I couldn't help (or resist) eavesdropping on, was obviously new. New guy was explaining how much he loves unhealthy Chinese food, but he also really wants to get super fit. So he begins explaining about this new home recipe he's discovered for General Tso's chicken that uses way less sugar. Nine minutes later, when my car arrived, he was *still* describing the dish and how it threads the needle between unshakeable cravings and fitness goals. And that is evangelism.

Everyone is preaching—whether it's antiracism, sexual liberation, democratic socialism, American nationalism, intermittent fasting, mindfulness meditation apps, new-wave psychedelics, the benefits of cold plunging, or food hacks for fitness junkies. And to borrow an insight from my friend John Mark Comer, all of these are gospels. They are messages about where hope lies, where the fullest kind of life is found, where community is formed, and how to become a better person.[8]

Everyone's preaching *a gospel*. Jesus' witnesses are simply those of us preaching *his gospel*. And the gospel of Jesus Christ goes something like this: There's an infinitely loving Creator who designed you for life so full you've only tasted it in drops. And his great passion is to heal and redeem you all the way through until you're swimming in that life. And he has supplied everything you need for full life and everlasting relationship with him. And he won't stop till the whole world is blanketed in heaven.

I mean, as far as news goes, "good" seems like a pretty conservative descriptor for all that, if you ask me.

Still, the very real tension remains. For his seventh birthday, my son Hank and I made an overnight trip up to Seattle to catch a Mariners game. He'd never been to a baseball game, and we went for the full experience—popcorn, hot dogs, and he even weaseled me into grossly overpaying for a jersey of his favorite player. On the way out when the game ended, there was a sidewalk preacher who'd set up a literal soapbox right outside the stadium. As we walked past, he belted into a bullhorn quoting Bible verses out of context and issuing a confusing collage of promises and warnings. That's what comes to the minds of many when they hear a word like "evangelism," and because that particular expression of "speaking about Jesus" is generally off-putting, many thoughtful, committed Jesus followers tend to dread and avoid evangelism altogether.

So maybe I could relieve a bit more of the tension by reminding you that evangelism is simply about being completely honest. Most of us have an allergic reaction to speaking about Jesus because we feel like we're selling something or working product placement into a genuine friendship. That's not it at all. People talk about what and who they love all the time—fashion, music, sports, a diet fad, a New Year's resolution, a potential promotion or job change.

To speak about the love of Jesus is not, first and foremost, to try to convince your coworkers of exclusive truth claims at the Friday evening happy hour. It's just being completely honest about your relationship to God in an environment where you're probably used to compartmentalizing your spirituality. To share about the growth, challenges, breakthroughs, and practices of your spiritual life freely. To invite others into your life of prayer, sabbath, and community. To live not manipulatively but honestly before all people, regardless of the setting. That's it.

In the last year, Quang, who lives a couple blocks over from our church in Portland, was intrigued to see a flood of young people pouring into a church building on Sunday mornings in the heart of what is statistically America's most unchurched and spiritually disinterested city. He and his family decided to check it out, and about eighteen months later, I was weeping as he and his nine-year-old daughter were baptized together in that very building.

Quang and I were reflecting on all this together on a walk around the neighborhood one afternoon when he casually mentioned that the night before he'd been at a wine bar just around the corner, catching up with a colleague he's known since university. After a couple hours together, when the place was near closing time, Quang said to his colleague, "Something really important has happened in my life I'd like to tell you about. I've become a follower of Jesus." And Quang explained the improbable series of events that led to him walking behind Jesus as Lord and Rabbi. He told his story. And nothing amazing happened, but neither was his friend put off or offended by it. He received it the way you receive anything when someone you respect and care for says, "I'd like to tell you about something really important that happened to me." A man stumbling through year one of discipleship to Jesus spoke love to a friend during last call, and a little wine bar on Broadway was flooded with heaven washing onto earth.

So there I am with my son, walking out of the Mariners game in downtown Seattle, listening to a preacher belt warnings and invitations into a bullhorn. As I reflect on it, the issue with this form of preaching the gospel is that it makes me think less about Jesus and more about the one doing the talking.

But when I heard Quang's story, the opposite happened. Somehow, Quang disappeared and all I could see was Jesus. Jesus there taking one last sip. Jesus paying the bill. And Jesus sharing vulnerably, bravely, and honestly with a colleague. And that's when we've gotten it right: when the way we speak about Jesus looks distinctly like the one we're speaking about.

In his book on the desert mothers and fathers, author Alan Jones writes, "Evangelism has been infected by the desire to package things for easy consumption . . . Jesus doesn't sell well except as a narcotic that will take away all your pain and make you intensely happy all the time. The question for the believer is how to tell the truth in faith so that what we are and what we present is both genuinely hopeful and uncompromisingly realistic."[9]

Speaking love isn't about finding the city's most crowded street corner with a bullhorn, and it's not about turning your every conversation into a trap where you're luring someone into the topic of the soul's eternal destiny. Speaking love is just about completely honest living. It's being your whole self equally in the disparate environments of your life—joys, struggles, practices, failures, and the sure place you rest your hope. Bringing your whole, honest self with you to worshiping at church, working at the office, running errands, parenting, visiting family, and sharing drinks with a friend. It's living your ordinary life while "telling the truth in a way that is both genuinely hopeful and uncompromisingly realistic." Living today like Jesus is King. That's witness.

Where are you living dishonestly? Where are you compartmentalizing your spirituality under the guise of being polite? Who do you think you're loving by hiding this part of you? I gently challenge you that while speaking up out of love for others might terrify you at first, it will make you more free and more alive in the end.

SUPERNATURAL LOVE

Summing up the life and ministry of Jesus, the apostle Peter said, "You know what has happened throughout the province of Judea, beginning in Galilee after the baptism that John preached—how God *anointed Jesus of Nazareth with the Holy Spirit and power*, and how he went around doing good and healing."[10] The miraculous ministry of Jesus, according to the Bible, came through the power of the Holy Spirit. An important note, given that Scripture also clearly claims that the same power we see in Jesus is promised to us in the same measure it was given to him.

We are a supernatural people, empowered to carry out Jesus' supernatural ministry of miraculous power, inexhaustible forgiveness, and vulnerability.

German theologian Jürgen Moltmann writes, "When Jesus expels demons and heals the sick, he is driving out of creation the powers of destruction, and is healing and restoring created beings who are hurt and sick. The lordship of God to which the healings witness, restores creation to health. Jesus's healings are not supernatural miracles in a natural world. They are the only truly 'natural' thing in a world that is unnatural, demonized and wounded."[11]

What I'm calling supernatural is simply living by the natural order of the Kingdom, and that's what witness is: to live in this world like Jesus is King.

The supernatural ministry of Jesus did occur in the temple from time to time. But unquestionably, the vast majority of supernatural snippets from the Gospels and the life of the church in Acts happened beyond the church walls in the context of ordinary life. Personally, my most memorable experiences of the Spirit's power have all been "in the wild." Holy Spirit ministry in the church is great, but it's great in the sense that a house cat is great—domesticated and cuddly. Holy Spirit ministry in the city is wild. It's scary in the sense that a bobcat is scary, but a bobcat is also a whole lot more powerful than a house cat.

Recently Kirsten was sitting at a sidewalk cafe with friends when Stan, a father we know from our kids' school, was walking past.

"Hey Stan, how's it going?" she asked.

He looked up, a little startled. "Uh, not good," he responded. In his surprise, he instinctively—and probably accidentally—responded with honesty. That very day his wife had left him. Without kids at home to tuck in that night, he didn't know what to do with himself, so he was out walking, surveying the wreckage of his life.

Kirsten invited Stan to sit with them and he did. She asked questions, creating space for him to share and process at his own pace. She prayed in the back of her mind the whole time, listened prophetically, and engaged supernaturally. Because what Stan definitely *didn't* need was a casually understated faith or a domesticated expression of love. What he needed was love that had claws, supernatural love that was scary but powerful. Love that wouldn't just lounge on his armchair but would hunt him down and wrestle him to the ground. And that is precisely why you and I have been filled with the Holy Spirit—so we can be his witnesses.

To love Stan with the supernatural love of Jesus in his moment of need required that Kirsten do something that, to her at least, felt unnatural. But if the Kingdom of God is reality, what felt unnatural to Kirsten was the only natural thing in our unnatural, demonized, wounded world. To live in this world as Jesus' witnesses requires that we get comfortable beyond our comfort zones.

There is just one simple requirement for being a witness: your eyes have to be open. If you were present at a crime scene but you were asleep when it went down, you're not a witness. Here is where you start in supernatural ministry: Every day, ask God to open your eyes to his invisible but invading Kingdom. "Open my eyes today at the office, at school, at book club tonight, at daycare pickup this afternoon, at the dog park with my neighbors this morning." Show up to your ordinary life supernaturally, by which I mean living by the laws that govern the Kingdom of heaven.

We are a supernatural people, and witness is the journey of discovering and embodying that. No one's ever said it quite like the great mystic saint Teresa of Avila: "Christ has no body now on earth but yours. Yours are the eyes with which he looks compassionately on this world. Yours are the feet with which he walks to do good. Yours are the hands with which he blesses all the world."[12]

SACRIFICIAL LOVE

While Jesus' body was a vessel for miraculous power, the most powerful use of Jesus' body came not by miraculous power but by humble sacrifice.

My friend Mike had had a particularly long week. He had to work late several nights, had a newborn at home, and had an endless barrage of demands on his time. So by Wednesday he was already booking a reservation and babysitter for a Friday evening out at his favorite spot to take a load off.

But it didn't work out that way. Mike's in recovery and working the steps. He and his sponsor are working through the Twelfth Step, which is all about the imperative of serving others. He'd made a commitment, for a specified period of time, to say yes to every invitation to serve that he was presented with. And that was particularly inconvenient when—in the middle of this long, hard week—he was invited to share his story at a local hospital for the severely mentally impaired that Friday night.

That's how Mike ended up not at a candlelit corner booth eating his favorite dish at his favorite restaurant, but at a linoleum table under fluorescent lighting across from a stranger so trapped in an illness that he couldn't even coherently speak, eating mashed-up peas and an unidentifiable meat substance. Keeping this gentleman company, mainly through eye contact, occasional physical touch, and a one-way conversation.

Relaying all this to me on the following Saturday morning, Mike said, "You know what's strange? Somehow, being there eating off that cafeteria tray with that man—being present with someone who only needs or wants the presence of a companion—it expanded my soul and filled me with refreshment and life in a way that fancy dinner I was daydreaming of never could've touched."

He went to that hospital thinking that these suffering people needed his service, but he discovered that it was actually the other way around. He needed that suffering man's presence. Because in his company, Mike encountered Jesus.

Sacrificial love is what Jesus modeled around a table the evening before Passover when he picked up a rag and started washing feet. And it's what Jesus carried out on a cross the following afternoon.

These days the miraculous ministry of the early church often gets all the press, but in their own time, the scandal of this new community that set the world on fire was their willingness to sacrifice. Supernatural expressions of love will always widen more eyes. And sacrificial acts of love will most often go unrecognized because sacrifice rarely makes an immediate, obvious impact. With sacrificial love there tends to be no big splash, no immediate result, no measurable return on investment.

Humble, hidden, sacrificial love is how we, too, can live as Jesus' witnesses. And as we do, something entirely upside down happens: We find the gratification and fulfillment we were chasing in all the wrong places.

The English "witness" is a common translation of the Greek word *martus*, which is also translated as "martyr."[13] To be Jesus' witness was virtually synonymous with being his martyr, losing one's life by association with him. But even apart from persecution, a sacrificial death to self (a martyrdom of sorts) has always been central to living as his witness. Jesus was the first witness, the first martyr, in this "upside-down, come alive by dying" Kingdom. And now he calls us to become like him.

As the years of your one, brief life fade, what will matter most profoundly is not your work, accomplishments, or reputation. All of that matters. But what will matter *most* is how you loved the people you got to live your days alongside. All our stories will get weighed on the scale of love.

What on that scale weighs heavy and what measures as light? Do your best to live accordingly today. That's witness.

THE BARGAIN OF A LIFETIME

Melanie heard fear in Jayla's voice. She was just a sixteen-year-old girl grappling with the loss of her mother, separation from her siblings, and adjustment to a new home all in the snap of a finger. Melanie and Ray didn't know how to help, how to order this chaos. But the Holy Spirit speaks over chaos to bring not just order but life. They prayed and waited on the Spirit. And it cost them everything.

In the wise words of Pete Greig, "Anyone who says that it is easy to follow Jesus is a liar. He Himself said that the way is narrow."[14] And that's exactly where Ray and Melanie find themselves today, trudging along the narrow way behind their Rabbi. It has cost them. But it has made them witnesses. And if given the chance to trade back this narrow way for a broader, more comfortable path and an easier, more predictable story, they'd never take it.

Greig continues, "But nothing we forgo in the cause of Christ—wealth, popularity, kudos, not even our very lives—can come anywhere close to the return. The price we pay to follow Jesus—whatever it might be—will acquire for us the most astounding 'bargain' of our lives!"[15]

Ray and Melanie aren't extraordinary. They're just witnesses.

And that's what the Holy Spirit offers all of us, provided we surrender everything—the bargain of a lifetime.

PRACTICE: SERVICE IN PURSUIT OF KINSHIP

The "witness" identity Jesus thrust on each of his followers and empowered them to become through the Holy Spirit should not be minimized to a single, particular expression. There's an endless array of expressions of witness based on the personality, gifts, environments, and opportunities of each individual.

That being said, we must also have a sustainable, rhythmic practice that permeates the whole of our lives with witness. Just as Sabbath is a one-day-a-week practice that informs the way we live day in and day out, and just as the evening Examen is a practice aimed at perceiving God's whisper at all times, so *service* is a particular, measurable, time-bound practice that helps us live at all times and in all places as witnesses.

Find somewhere to regularly practice service to those in need in your city or community. I'm talking about things like volunteering at the women's shelter, becoming a foster parent, or providing aid and care to a local refugee. If you do not regularly practice service to those in need in your local area, something essential is missing in your discipleship to Jesus, and it is highly unlikely that you'll grow in your God-given identity as his witness.

Once you have established a rhythm of service, be sure you engage in service *in pursuit of kinship*. Kinship is what distinguishes Jesus' vision of justice from every other. Most secular definitions of justice end with a need met. Those with extra bread give some of theirs to those who lack. This is good, but it keeps the roles of service provider and service recipient intact. Jesus' definition of justice does not end with a need met but with a family restored. While it may begin with the plentiful sharing with the lacking, the ultimate goal is for the plentiful and the poverty-stricken to break bread together, seated as equals, at Jesus' table.

Why do we serve others? Not because it works, necessarily. Anyone who has ever engaged in the practice of service knows that results vary. We serve because the fearfully and wonderfully made people we serve are worth it. To spend ourselves on others, to enter into their suffering, that is our reward.

There are two types of action—action *for* and action *from*. Action *for* is done for a desired end, and that motivation dominates Western culture. Invest time, money, or labor to get something back in return. Action *from*, on the other hand, is done not to achieve a desired end but *from* a conviction. I invest my time, money, or labor because I've been freely given more than I'll ever be able to give away.

The work of service in the Kingdom of God is action *from*, and that means results will vary. But the service is always worth it.

ELEVEN

REDEMPTIVE SUFFERING

The Spirit you received brought about your adoption to sonship. And by him we cry, "Abba, Father." The Spirit himself
testifies with our spirit that we are God's children. Now if we
are children, then we are heirs—heirs of God and co-heirs
with Christ, if indeed we share in his sufferings in order that
we may also share in his glory.

ROMANS 8:15–17

"WE'VE GOTTA GET SOMETHING in your stomach," Robin
implored. "Could you manage just a couple bites of a granola bar?"

I was staring at a blinking cursor and blank page. Computer
sitting open on my lap. Unable to get the room to stop spinning,
let alone think straight enough to string together words in coherent
sequence.

Robin is the amazing nurse assigned to my care for today, my
fifth consecutive day of chemotherapy. I'm too nauseous to eat,
but the lack of food in my body is causing a reaction to the poison
cocktail they're drip feeding me through the port in my chest,

just below my collarbone. I'm being fed a combination of toxins dangerous enough the nurse has to wrap herself in the medical equivalent of a hazmat suit to handle the plastic bags holding liters of liquid that flow right into my arteries. These drugs are killing me slowly, but—thankfully—first they're killing the cancer that's killing me quickly.

A couple weeks prior to my diagnosis, I'd facilitated a workshop for thousands in the Portland Convention Center, where we prayed for miraculous healing, practiced the prophetic, and celebrated the power of the Holy Spirit manifested through the miraculous events that followed. I led a workshop on the power of the Holy Spirit to heal through the prayers of God's people— all the while unaware that two malignant tumors swelled in my stomach, reaching the most advanced stage, requiring immediate treatment with an aggressive form of chemo.

And now, amid battling chemo's impact on my mind and body, I find myself writing about redemptive suffering.

As I choke down a nibble of the granola bar, I'm firmly aware that to be this sick today is actually a great gift. Just a generation ago, I'd have died a young man, life cut short in my mid-thirties, leaving behind the woman I promised to grow old with and three little boys I never got to see come of age.

Still, on this early March Friday, as snow flurries drift down on the street outside, I'm also firmly aware that I'm the youngest patient at an oncology unit I'll visit regularly for the remainder of my many days—best-case scenario.

My situation is both common and unique.

On the one hand, to be human is to suffer. In my short life I have stood over the caskets of the old and the young, peeling open the Scriptures to offer words of consolation to crowded funeral parlors grieving the elderly taken at an expected but no-less-tragic age, the young snatched from among us in a gasp, and even infants we barely got to know. I have wept with those reeling from a diagnosis, sat in stunned silence in the wake of a friend's brain aneurysm, and prayed with many would-be parents in the quiet grief of miscarriage. I have known the suffering victims of abuse, trauma, and tragedy. And, of course, I am such a victim myself. The sad truth is that the experience of suffering is common to every human life.

Suffering is always looming, always nipping at our heels, occasionally wrestling us to the ground. Some of us never get up. And even those who do walk with a limp. Suffering tends to be both where we look hardest for God and where God is most difficult to find. As Cistercian monk Thomas Keating wrote, "In the dark nights . . . the rituals and practices that previously supported our faith and devotion, fail us. Faith becomes simply belief in God's goodness without any test of it. It is trusting in God without knowing whom we are trusting, because the relationship we thought we had with God has disappeared."[1]

While suffering is common to all people, suffering is also unique to each individual. As Tolstoy famously observed in *Anna Karenina*, we each suffer in our own particular way. Suffering cannot and should not be measured or compared. Suffering cannot and should not be dismissed as inevitable or swept under the rug in general. Because while everyone in history has suffered, no one has ever suffered as you've suffered.

The most natural human response to this inconvenient truth is, of course, to do our best to avoid suffering. And, when suffering rudely intrudes on our lives, we do our best to minimize its effects. It is striking, then, that the biblical narrative takes a decidedly alternative view.

GLORY IN OUR SUFFERINGS

The apostle Paul, no stranger to suffering, offers a surprising take: "We also glory in our sufferings, because we know that suffering produces perseverance; perseverance, character; and character, hope. And hope does not put us to shame, because God's love has been poured out into our hearts through the Holy Spirit, who has been given to us."[2]

Suffering may be many things, but glorious?

The indwelling power of the Holy Spirit, both in the story of Scripture and the life of the believer, means holding the wonder of the miraculous and the tragedy of suffering in tension. That's a tension that has, understandably, caused many to storm out of a healing prayer seminar, scream angry prayers at God through tears, and throw a book like this one against a wall.

It is striking, then, that the very tension many find unbearable is celebrated on the pages of the New Testament—most prominently in the writings of Paul. His sentiment in Romans 5, connecting the experience of human suffering to the power of the Holy Spirit, is not an anomaly but a pattern in his letters. Nearly verbatim statements are made elsewhere in the letters to the Roman, Corinthian, and Philippian churches.[3]

So what are we missing that the ancients knew about the power of the Holy Spirit amid the injustice of suffering? How on earth does suffering connect to glory? And, most personally for me, what does the presence and power of the Holy Spirit mean, not in the peak moment of encounter in the closing moments of a worship gathering, but right here and now where I sit as I write these words—in the chemotherapy infusion unit of the hospital, stomach turning with nausea, room spinning, eyes struggling to focus?

The Holy Spirit fills us with resurrection power to live in the "already" Kingdom right now. And the same Holy Spirit fills us with redemptive patience to bear with the suffering of the "not yet" Kingdom we still await. The best-kept secret about the Holy Spirit is that his power is just as living, active, and present in our suffering as it is in our triumphs. In fact, as impossible as it may be to believe, the biblical portrait of the Holy Spirit is so intimate and dignifying that not an ounce of suffering from even one of his children will be for naught. All the pain we face is repurposed by the Spirit as a key ingredient in the redemption of the world.

But to bring that idea from the cloudy place of theology and ground it in the actual place of day-to-day life requires a look at the biblical story through a forgotten lens.

SATAN, THE AUTHOR
OF SUFFERING

The biblical story does not begin with conflict, but union. In contrast with every other ancient Near Eastern creation story, Genesis begins with goodness, not violence or suffering. God did not create a world of pain but a place he called "good" every step of the way and "very good" when his work was done. He created people to live in paradise, the union of heaven and earth, apart from death, grief, sadness, and pain.

Turn just a single page, though, and God's very good creation was corrupted by a deceiver. God told one story. The serpent told another. Humanity believed the serpent, and the world as we know it is the product of the lie our ancestors believed. As my friend Pete Hughes often says, "The story you live *in* is the story you live *out*." All of our trouble is the product of a curse that infected every aspect of God's good world.

Why do we weep over caskets? Why would a life begin in a mother's womb only to die there before he or she lives a single day? Why does a tsunami wave wash over the coast of Indonesia or a hurricane ram into the heart of New Orleans? Why does a disease in one person in Wuhan spread until the whole world is paralyzed? Not because God willed any of it, but because the consequences of this curse are of the furthest-reaching variety.

Please don't misunderstand me. I'm not saying that all suffering is the direct result of any individual's particular sin. I'm saying that living outside of Eden has consequences. Death and sin have infected the very world we live in, and all suffering is a symptom of sin (the world we chose) not God (the good world he created).

Many ask the "why" question to God about suffering, and that's an important question. It's not the *only* question, though. There's a second, equally important question that colors and shapes the first. "How does God *feel* about suffering?" Genesis chapter 6 gives the answer: "The LORD saw how great the wickedness of the human race had become on the earth, and that every inclination of the thoughts of the human heart was only evil all the time. The LORD regretted that he had made human beings on the earth, and his heart was deeply troubled."[4]

God looked at the consequences of sin—the way people treated each other; the thoughts that ran through our neural pathways; the mixed motives, manipulation, and selfish intentions within us; the suffering it all produced as history rolled by—and he "regretted" making creation in the first place. God's elation in Genesis 1 is matched by his grief in Genesis 6.

Suffering grieves God's heart. It grieves his heart even more than it grieves mine or yours.

No wonder, then, that God's presence and power is especially focused on those who suffer—the poor, the oppressed, the marginalized. He's our father, and every loving parent is quick to give care to a child in crisis. Legend has it that Susanna Wesley, mother to famed revivalists John and Charles Wesley, was once asked which of her nineteen children she loved the most. Her immediate response was, "The one who is sick, lost, hurting, or forgotten." God is a parent whose heart is disproportionately drawn to the suffering child.

But God doesn't merely grieve or offer sympathy for our suffering from a safe distance. He enters into it.

JESUS, THE SUFFERING REDEEMER

Jesus' ministry began when the Holy Spirit descended on him in the form of a dove at his baptism. But the Spirit did not first empower Jesus with authoritative teaching or miraculous spectacle; instead, the Spirit led Jesus into intercessory suffering. "Jesus, full of the Holy Spirit, left the Jordan and was led by the Spirit into the wilderness, where for forty days he was tempted by the devil."[5] Jesus, anointed by the Spirit, squared off against humanity's deceiver and prevailed.

Satan's three temptations—turning stones into bread, enlisting angels to rescue him, and worshiping Satan in exchange for regaining dominion over this fallen world—were all about shortcuts. Taste bread without tilling the soil, planting a seed, and waiting. Win instant popularity through spectacle. Get your creation back without suffering. Become a King without ever becoming a servant. Wear a crown without ever carrying a cross. Why didn't Jesus take the shortcut? Because a victorious but unsuffering God is not good news.

Human beings are meaning-seeking creatures. We weave narratives that integrate the events of our lives into a coherent whole, a plot. And suffering is the greatest disturbance to our self-storytelling. Psychologist David Benner writes, "Ultimately, we need a meaning strong enough to make suffering sufferable. This is the crucial test of any life meaning. . . . [It] has to help us cope with suffering."[6]

The most scandalous part of Jesus to ancient ears was that he, the Lord, would suffer.

God on a throne? Sure.

A God who bleeds? A God who weeps? A God who grieves? Unthinkable.

I understand why it's such a shock that God would suffer, but I also think that a God who doesn't suffer probably isn't a God worth trusting. Without the courage to crawl down into this world and feel the darkness with the same helplessness as the rest of us, how could God be trusted? How could he be relatable? Without suffering, how could God tell a story deep enough to hold our own suffering?

Jesus, and only Jesus, makes suffering sufferable. Through his own suffering he looks both you and me in the eye in the midst of our suffering. He's winning a decisive victory, and he's doing it by bearing the cost of the curse, by enduring the real-life experience of a sin-infected creation.

Jesus' suffering culminated at the cross. He was crucified outside the city gate, the ancient equivalent to skid row, an unpoliced urban ghetto. The uncivilized, the criminal, the sick, and the weak were cast out of the city beyond the gate. Cast off as something less than human, animals in the wild to fend for themselves. The Word made flesh, God in human form, carried his cross beyond that gate, executed as a common criminal.

Ultimately, it wasn't Jesus' life that died beyond the city gate; it was our sin. It was suffering's grip on the world that was put in a tomb, never to rise.

THE POWER OF THE HOLY SPIRIT IN JESUS' SUFFERING

At every moment in the story of God incarnate, it is the Holy Spirit who dignifies Jesus' suffering, making his suffering substitutionary, repurposing his suffering powerfully for the redemption of all creation.

Who drove Jesus into the wilderness to be tempted, to resist the very temptation that each and every one of us fails to resist, which is the source of all this suffering in the first place? The Holy Spirit.

Who enlivened Jesus' body with a resurrection life that not even the cruelty of crucifixion could overcome? The Holy Spirit.

And throughout Jesus' ministry, he promised that same Spirit to us—with increasing frequency the nearer he got to the pinnacle of his suffering.

The Spirit is the Comforter present with us in our suffering.

The Spirit is the Advocate redeeming our suffering. The Spirit is the Counselor guiding us through the processing and healing of our wounds. The Spirit enables us to continue the cruciform ministry of Jesus, suffering in love on behalf of others.

THE POWER OF THE HOLY SPIRIT IN MY SUFFERING

So here I sit, not at the coffee shop counter where the majority of this book has been written, but instead in a reclined hospital chair, meds dripping into my bloodstream, shivering under a blanket and typing much slower than usual. What does the presence and power of the Holy Spirit mean right here and now?

This side of the serpent's deception, we do not get a choice in our suffering as God works to re-create the world in his image. We do, however, get to choose what our suffering *does to us.*

The story you live *in* is the story you live *out,* so we are given more than just the life of Christ as a model for redemptive suffering. We are given the Holy Spirit to make us suffering redeemers like Jesus. *I* am filled—personally—with the Holy Spirit to make *my* suffering redemptive, even glorious.

But how does that actually work? How does suffering produce glory when we're not reading it on a page but experiencing it in real life? A diagnosis, a loss, an interruption, a betrayal—how is any of that connected to glory? There's nothing intrinsically noble about suffering. Sometimes pain just hurts, suffering is just sad, and grief just has to be gotten through. Sentimentalizing the bad in our lives doesn't make it good. It's still bad, plain and simple.

But the Holy Spirit works with both the good and bad in our lives for renewal, so let's wring out the ways—as far as we can define them—that the Holy Spirit not only dignifies our experience but repurposes the atrocity of suffering into the creative force of redemption. Suffering is connected to glory because suffering—like nothing else in this life—avails us the opportunity to become like Jesus in this chaotic and corrupted world. The Holy Spirit is at work not only in our mountaintop moments but also (and often most profoundly) in the valley of the shadow of death, converting our surrendered suffering into *love, compassion, gratitude, groaning,* and, ultimately, *redemption*.

Love

Suffering exposes our weakness and fragility, and that, when offered to others, is both an act of love and an invitation to be loved.

For three years Jesus' disciples knew him as always active, always doing. He was befriending the friendless and agitating the establishment, feeding the five thousand and opening the eyes of the blind, welcoming the stranger and teaching the masses. Jesus was a man on a mission, face set like flint toward Jerusalem. And through this activity, he was offering love and being loved by others.

But in his final twenty-four hours, there was an obvious change in cadence. Every gospel author significantly slows the narrative. Jesus' supernatural activity is replaced by a willed passivity.[7] He was arrested, questioned, whipped, and mocked. He was helped in carrying his cross. He was nailed down to it. Jesus, a beacon of loving strength for three years, now offered that same love in his weakness.

By not only showing us his triumphant weakness on the cross but his suffering weakness in the journey to the cross, Jesus made space for love. Without a weak Jesus, Peter, James, and John would not get invited to pray with him in friendship at Gethsemane. Without weakness, the women would not get to gather in loyal, present love at the cross after nearly all the other disciples had scattered. It was Jesus' prolonged weakness that afforded Mary the opportunity to hear her son's concern for her when he asked John to care for his widowed mother as if she were John's own mother.

Jesus' weakness is an offering of love to others and, equally, offers space for others to love him in a way that they could not love him in his strength.

I can identify with that part of Christ at present. I am, perhaps to a fault, a man on a mission—but in this season of weakness I am learning to love and receive love in new ways. The very people who have walked beside me in my strength, companioning me in wide-eyed and wonderstruck adventures of mission, are loving me in very different ways in my weakness.

Morgan has held me, weeping harder than I have for my body's suffering. Bethany, Gavin, Casey, and Jarin have all offered unique gifts, symbols that help me hold on to hope in the long, dark days. Kate, Bri, and Sarah have organized meals for my family. Christian, Yinka, and Karen were there to help me muster a celebration at the close of the first treatment cycle. Ashlee, without me even asking, has been doing the yard work I lack the strength to do. Andrew helped me assemble my son's birthday present I lacked the strength to piece together on my own. Kirsten has sat with me every minute of the journey. And here sits Peter, turning another page, reading and praying the Psalms over me in the infusion room when I don't have the strength to pray.

Paul tells us that "hope does not put us to shame, because God's love has been poured out into our hearts through the Holy Spirit, who has been given to us."[8] This oft-referenced and deeply true expression of the Spirit's power is nearly always taken on its own, but it's worth remembering that, when Paul wrote it, he framed this Spirit-empowered outpouring of love in the context of our suffering. Suffering exposes our weakness—the very weakness we can offer to others in love and through which we can receive love. The ways God pours his love into our hearts through the Holy Spirit are as beautiful and varied as the turning of a kaleidoscope. But nowhere does the Spirit meet us more profoundly with the experiential, transformational love of God than in the weakness exposed by suffering.

Compassion

Properly endured, suffering gives way to compassion, which is a frequent descriptor of the character of Yahweh in the Hebrew Bible. In fact, our English word "compassion," traced to its origins, literally means "co-suffer." To be compassionate is to willingly enter into the suffering of another.

In the early stages of suffering, the sufferer sees only his or her own situation. There's a kind of tunnel vision produced—a normal human reaction. With time, though, some can rise above their suffering and begin to see others through it. Their own pain is repurposed toward an otherwise impossible compassion for the suffering of others.

I was lucky enough to spend a couple years in a group mentorship program with the late Dr. Timothy Keller in my early years in pastoral ministry. One Thursday afternoon, before we walked alongside one another to the subway stop on the Upper West Side, he candidly shared with a handful of us about his own cancer journey. "Since receiving my diagnosis," he reflected, "I keep thinking of all the people I pastored over the years who went through cancer. I wasn't rude. I just didn't think a whole lot about it because it's such a common disease. But now that my life is hanging in the balance at the expense of that very disease, and I'm going to all these treatments and feeling the effects of all these drugs, I can't believe I responded to such a painful, personal, prolonged disruption as if it were routine."

Losing your mother creates empathy for anyone else who has lost their mother. Experiencing miscarriage and infertility creates empathy for anyone else who has lived the same. Being diagnosed with bipolar disorder softens the heart toward others suffering from mental illness. Living off ramen noodles to make rent softens the heart toward the poor. There's an inherent solidarity in suffering that draws compassion to the surface.

Suffering is never welcome, always an intruder. But once suffering has kicked our door down, it offers us an invitation: to see through eyes of compassion and to share in the glory of Christ by entering into the suffering of others. Whether we like it or not, we are going to share in the world's sufferings. Suffering is not evenly distributed—we all suffer in different ways and to varying degrees. Will our share in the world's suffering embitter us or soften us, close us off or open us up?

And here we encounter the Holy Spirit: when we respond to suffering's invitation by growing in co-suffering—compassion. The Spirit empowers us to relieve another's suffering by intentionally entering into and sharing their pain. Our prayers for the suffering of others take on a newfound depth and urgency. The Holy Spirit is the generative force breathing divine power on our prayers and redeeming our suffering for the sake of others.

Gratitude

Suffering is the scale that reveals what's real and counterfeit in our lives. A diagnosis or world-altering phone call can reveal that life's lesser worries aren't the heavy burdens we thought they were. Conversely, that same diagnosis or phone call can reveal that things we often take for granted and de-prioritize are actually life's great treasures. Suddenly, conversation with a loved one, waking up tomorrow morning next to a spouse, tucking a child in at night, or the familiar embrace of a friend go from thoughtless to priceless.

British singer-songwriter Nick Cave has lost two children. His son Jethro was found dead of undisclosed causes in a motel room in Melbourne, Australia, at the age of thirty-one. This came seven years after his fifteen-year-old son, Arthur, tragically died when he fell from a cliff near their family's home in Brighton, England. Grief is a primary theme explored in Cave's memoir, in which he writes,

> Sometimes I try to bring to mind what Arthur has given
> to me, not just when he was alive but in his absence, too,
> almost as a way of finding meaning in the hopelessness that

descends from time to time. And the truth is that Arthur's passing ultimately became a motivating force, so that, over the years, Susie and I have experienced some very beautiful, meaningful things in our lives, truly beautiful things, and in many ways they lead like a powder trail directly back to Arthur's death. This is the secret, terrible beauty at the heart of loss, of grief. Of course, we would give it all back if we could see him again, but those cosmic deals are not to be made . . . In the light of that knowledge, we find gratitude to be a simple and essential act.[9]

So often, life's deepest goods become routine, easily pushed to the side in order to finish an assignment or schedule one more meeting or prepare tomorrow's presentation. Times of comfort lead us into distraction, to a place where we gradually put our greatest treasures on the back burner. But suffering, endured thoughtfully, accurately weighs life's priorities and instills gratitude for the things that truly matter.

Groaning

Paul tells us that "the whole creation has been groaning as in the pains of childbirth right up to the present time." He says further that "we ourselves, who have the firstfruits of the Spirit, groan inwardly as we wait eagerly for our adoption to sonship, the redemption of our bodies."[10]

Creation groans and so do we. Groaning is an expression of pain, but the type of groaning that we do in this life is labor pain groaning. Though the pain is very real, it's also a very good sign. A laboring woman's groans accompany the contractions that eventually result in the birth of a child. Similarly, those filled with the Holy Spirit are pregnant with the new life of the Spirit, and that means that even the suffering we experience in this world—the "groaning as in the pains of childbirth"—points to the promise of new life: a world without suffering, when God will wipe away every tear from our eyes, shelter us in his loving presence, and redeem every pain we've ever felt.

Sometimes suffering functions like a record scratch in our spiritual lives, silencing our conversation with a God we suddenly don't recognize, don't understand, don't know if we can trust. When suffering threatens to silence our prayer lives, the Spirit remains active. Paul continues in Romans 8, "In the same way, the Spirit helps us in our weakness. We do not know what we ought to pray for, but the Spirit himself intercedes for us through wordless groans. And he who searches our hearts knows the mind of the Spirit, because the Spirit intercedes for God's people in accordance with the will of God."[11] The Holy Spirit indwelling us prays both *through us* and *for us* in the midst of our suffering.

In the wake of an interruption so startlingly painful you don't know what to say to the God you would've given anything to if he'd just prevented it, you can only let out a groan. A loud, angry, pain-stricken groan. And somehow the Holy Spirit within you is so present and active that he translates that groan into the requests for what you really need. In your deepest pain he ushers you into the very presence of the Father, turning your wordless groaning into communion.

The groaning of the Holy Spirit is an acknowledgment of God's presence in our deepest places of pain, loss, alienation, and grief. In some mysterious way that is nearly impossible to explain apart from shared experience, suffering often begins as the experience of God's absence but can be transformed into the place we feel and sense God's presence and love most acutely. Because we have a God who did not shy away from suffering, it can become the crucible in which we know his love most personally and profoundly.

The Holy Spirit is present and powerful not just in miraculous interventions or mountaintop moments. He can be heard groaning in shocked hospital rooms and overcrowded orphanages, in the tearing open of an eviction notice, in the reading of a suicide note. Yes, the power of the Holy Spirit sounds like the gasps of wonder as Lazarus emerges from his tomb. But the power of the same Spirit is heard also in the wails, sobs, and righteous anger erupting from the grieving, asking for it all to come to an end, for all to be made right, for the full redemption promised by King Jesus.

Redemption

I have a scar on my knee from the slip I took in a neighbor's creek during an all-in sprint to win capture the flag on a humid July day when I was twelve years old. Another scar sits above my left eye from the friendly push that sent me careening into a table corner, courtesy of the boy behind me in the snack line at Vacation Bible School when I was nine. A scar sits just below my right collarbone where the port was inserted to aid in my first rounds of chemotherapy following a very unexpected, life-threatening cancer diagnosis at thirty-six. Three scars telling three very different stories.

I remember nights when I was a kid, lying on my parents' bed with a nearly empty bowl of Neapolitan ice cream next to me, watching I Love Lucy reruns with my dad. He lay on his back, his head on a stack of pillows. I lay on my stomach, head supported by my hands, elbows resting on the mattress. There, head to toe nearly every time, I was fascinated by the calluses on his toes. "Why is your skin so tough here, Dad? Your pinkie toe is sharpened like a blade."

That moment leaped to my imagination recently when Simon, my six-year-old son, asked me the identical question in a nearly identical moment. Over the years, and the many steps taken, I'd traded places with my father. Now it was my feet carrying wounds of a sort with a story behind them.

As a boy I was fascinated by my grandfather's drooping skin from his chin to his neck. "Why do you have extra skin here, Pops? Did someone stretch it out?" I'm sure he loved the question. The wrinkles that form on our foreheads and in creases around our eyes tell a story of days gone by, thousands of days collecting even more moments that make up a life, and no amount of Botox keeps our faces from telling the long tale.

The wounds we carry on our bodies are storytellers. Wrinkles tell the story of the days we've lived and the days we've endured. Calluses tell the story of the steps we've walked through green pastures and death valleys alike. Scars tell the stories of the hurts we've felt, the pain we've endured, the tears we've cried, and the blood we've shed.

John Donne was the pastor of St. Paul's Cathedral in central London in the sixteenth century. He was also a literary giant and influential poet. His most famous work, though, is a private journal published after his death under the title *Devotions*. Donne pastored St. Paul's through the bubonic plague, a pandemic that ravaged the European world, killing up to an estimated 50 percent of the continent's population. Donne lay sick for months on what seemed certain to be his deathbed, his congregation scattered and quarantined.

As the news broke of my own cancer diagnosis, a friend offered me an updated version of *Devotions* as a gift, and I used Donne's prayers as a guide for my own journey of suffering. There's one famous entry in *Devotions* that serves as a hinge point in the journal: Donne listens to the sound of funeral bells outside as he lies on his sickbed inside. He imagines they're his own bells, imagines his own funeral. And as he does, he moves from fighting against his suffering—grasping for relief, for some kind of escape or change of circumstance—to submitting to his suffering. His prayers shift—the first half of them all pleas that his pain be removed, the second half pleas that his pain be redeemed.

My journey isn't so different. At the start of chemo, I was counting down the rounds, managing the side effects, clinging to life as I knew it before my diagnosis in every way I could, anticipating the return of that life with each passing day. As chemo progressed I thought less and less about the end, even about the outcome, and more about what I wanted to be true of me when I came out of this wilderness.

Saint John of the Cross wrote in the sixteenth century, "The best fruit grows in land that is cold and dry." At some point in my own journey, I stopped daydreaming about subverting the suffering, and I submitted to the formative process of suffering. I stopped praying for removal of pain and started praying for redemption of pain.

Philip Yancey created a modern rendering of John Donne's *Devotions*. In his own conclusion reflecting on Donne's life of illness, Yancey—suffering from Parkinson's disease and increasingly feeling the effects—reflected on his own life.

> In my writing career, I have interviewed US presidents, rock stars, professional athletes, actors, and other celebrities. I have also profiled leprosy patients in India, pastors imprisoned for their faith in China, women rescued from sex trafficking, parents of children with rare genetic disorders, and many who suffer from diseases far more debilitating than Parkinson's. Reflecting on the two groups, here's what stands out: With some exceptions, those who live with pain and failure tend to be better stewards of their life circumstances than those who live with success and pleasure. Pain redeemed impresses me more than pain removed.[12]

No one chooses to suffer, and no own escapes the crucible of suffering unchanged. We do not get to choose whether we will suffer or even how we will suffer. We only get to choose, by our response, if the suffering that rudely intrudes on our lives will make us more or make us less. "We think the becoming more like God means becoming more powerful and protected from pain," writes psychologist Curt Thompson. "When in fact it is in our suffering— and in our persevering in the face of it in vulnerable community . . . that we actually become more and more like God."[13]

The rest of that balmy July afternoon after I fell in the neighbor's creek while playing capture the flag was spent in the emergency room. By the time the sun was setting, I'd returned to the neighbor's backyard to show off my new stitches. We all huddled together comparing scars, swapping stories of pain endured and valor won.

After his resurrection, Jesus appeared to his disciples, and the scene was not unlike boys swapping scar stories: "See my hands, my feet. Touch my scars. Run your hands over my healed wounds—over the hurt I've felt, pain I've endured, tears I've cried, blood I've shed." The miraculous ministry of Jesus introduced us to a God with the power and compassion to remove pain. The sacrificial death of Jesus introduced us to a God who, even when he doesn't remove pain, always redeems it. Because of Jesus' scars, all of my suffering and yours becomes a scar—hurt healed, pain whose sting is gone, tears wiped away, bleeding stopped. Because of Jesus, all pain, all suffering is redeemed. Provided that I, like a boy by the neighbor's creek, hold out my scars and respond, "Here, Jesus, are my hands, my feet."

Aaron Kushner was diagnosed as a toddler with a very rare disease that would prevent him from ever growing taller than three feet, ever growing hair on his head, and, worst of all, ever reaching adulthood. Aaron died at just fourteen.

His father Harold, a Jewish rabbi, reflecting on his experience of grief, wrote,

> I am a more sensitive person, a more effective pastor, a more
> sympathetic counselor because of Aaron's life and death than
> I would ever have been without it. And I would give up all of
> those gains in a second if I could have my son back. If I could
> choose, I would forego all the spiritual growth and depth

which has come my way because of our experiences, and be what I was fifteen years ago, an average rabbi, an indifferent counselor, helping some people and unable to help others, and the father of a bright, happy boy. But I cannot choose.[14]

Given the choice that none of us have, I imagine we'd all take the same trade. One of the great dignities the Holy Spirit offers us amid suffering is the way it has the potential to forge our character into the image of Jesus. All of that is very real and very good, but it's also not enough. *Love, compassion, gratitude,* and *groaning* are all wonderful, but, on their own, they're still not enough. And that's why the biblical story doesn't only dignify suffering in the present but promises its decisive defeat in the future:

> Look! God's dwelling place is now among the people, and he will dwell with them. They will be his people, and God himself will be with them and be their God. He will wipe every tear from their eyes. There will be no more death or mourning or crying or pain, for the old order of things has passed away.[15]

Suffering, for those who accept the free gift of God's grace, does not win. It does not have the final word. The curse that infected creation will be fully, finally, forever eradicated. That's the end of the story, the full realization of Jesus' victory. But we're not to the end yet. We're still right in the thick of the plot, living in the consequences of the conflict, but tasting the fruit of the victory.

God doesn't promise to protect us from pain. In fact, he promises we'll feel it. But he does promise to redeem every moment of pain. He doesn't just promise that, in the end, suffering won't win. He promises that every bit of suffering you endure in this life will be woven by the great storyteller into the tapestry of redemption. That every heartbreak, loneliness, abandonment, trial, and tragedy will be redeemed and made into a piece of the creative force through which redemption comes. God is building the promised heavenly city out of the shattered pieces of the fall.

Miraculous power and redemptive suffering are both the work of the Holy Spirit. And both bring heaven to earth. "I want to know Christ—yes, to know the power of his resurrection and participation in his sufferings, becoming like him in his death, and so, somehow, attaining to the resurrection from the dead."[16] This side of the resurrection, suffering is a part of our inheritance as Spirit-filled people.

The Holy Spirit empowers us not to escape suffering but to endure it—and even to repurpose it into a key ingredient in the recipe of redemption. The Spirit of the living God within you and me makes suffering sufferable.

PRACTICE: LAMENT

Lament is the practice of groaning with the Spirit in the midst of suffering—my own suffering or the suffering of another. Lament is an active groan, practiced individually or communally. It is most frequently encompassed in the repeated biblical phrase, "How long, O Lord?" Essentially, this is a shorthand cry for full redemption. "How long will I live on mustard seeds of the Kingdom awaiting the full reality? How long will I bear this pain awaiting King Jesus to bring it to an end? How long will God's people suffer in a half-redeemed world fraught with injustice, oppression, and pain?"

Lament is all over the Bible, making up about 40 percent of the psalms that serve as the prayer book for God's people, but lament is mostly absent in the modern church. The unintended consequence is that many modern disciples do not know how to talk to God in the wake of suffering. This leads to silence in our lives in the very circumstances that the Holy Spirit and God's holy people historically grew loudest in their groans.

Why is lament significant though? Who really wants to pray and sing about suffering? Lament is significant because *it names and personalizes suffering*. We cannot groan with the Spirit in our own pain or enter into the pain of another if suffering has no name and face. In the simple, wise words of Harold S. Kushner, "There are many things that can only be seen through eyes that have cried."[17]

Lament begins with taking stock of the gap between my present and God's promised future. To lament is to willingly look to and name the redemption I still await, the redemption a loved one still awaits, or the redemption our world still awaits.

When we name that awaited redemption in the most honest terms possible, we mature beyond mere reaction. This is why lament prayers are often put to poetry and song in the Psalms; poetry and melody force a deeply processed, slowly written, and artfully crafted reflection. This is not an unintelligible rant, though it may start there. Instead, it's a well-crafted, brutally honest plea for God's accelerated redemption in the place of present suffering.

Lament globally over war-torn nations, powerless refugees, and impoverished villages. Lament locally over systemic inequalities, injustices, and problems affecting fearfully and wonderfully made people—problems that need more than just a new political policy to fix. Lament personally over your own illness, loneliness, abuse, and pain. Pray exactly like you think you aren't allowed to, and pray that way long enough and slow enough to craft the language of your current pain and future longing. That's lament.

Theologian and author Soong-Chan Rah points out that, biblically, there are two types of lament—eulogies and hospital visits.

A eulogy, the words spoken at a funeral, are laments *with no hope* this side of eternity. A eulogy merely puts grief in its proper context. That's mostly what you'll find in the book of Lamentations.

A hospital visit is grief *with hope* because there's still the possibility of healing. When you visit someone suffering in the hospital, there's undeniable pain you face and confront when you walk into their room. But a eulogy would be entirely inappropriate because there's still a heartbeat and breath in those lungs. There is a variety of lament that comes with hope, and that's mostly what you'll find in the Psalms.[18]

Because of Jesus, every lament for the believer is ultimately a hospital visit. The groans of the Holy Spirit within us are laments with hope. Because we have a Redeemer who keeps his promises, we grieve, wail, and groan in the in-between, but we do all of it with hope.

TWELVE

THE WAY OF LOVE

Follow the way of love and eagerly desire gifts of the Spirit.

1 CORINTHIANS 14:1

MY PATERNAL GRANDMOTHER, EVELYN, is ninety-one years old. She was born fourth in a family of five girls. She hardly got to know her mother, who passed away when she was only three years old. Her father fought in World War II, where he was exposed to some of the fiercest combat faced by American troops. He returned from war with a drinking problem he hadn't taken with him when he left. It was bad enough that Evelyn moved out of the house at just thirteen to live with her older sister. She married Teddy, my grandfather, at twenty years old. She had six children, who she raised on a tobacco farm in rural Kentucky, less than twenty miles from the house she was born in. To make ends meet, she worked full time in a nearby shirt factory, where she sewed buttons and seams all day, every day for more than thirty years.

Evelyn has hardly traveled. She's never left the country, only put her feet in the ocean a couple of times, and not laid eyes on much of the world outside the small patch of it she was born onto. She has spent her entire life in a twenty-mile radius, the last seventy years of it on the same few acres of Kentucky farmland she woke up to this morning.

I am one of her twenty-plus grandchildren. I have lived in five US states and sixteen different homes. I have put my toes in three of the world's oceans. I have traveled to five continents and a number of different countries. And I've only been alive a handful of years longer than the years she punched the clock in that shirt factory. I guess, by our culture's definition, all that makes me "cultured" and Evelyn something else.

But I wonder, What makes a person deep? What are the conditions in which the human soul grows up?

ALL TOGETHER IN ONE PLACE

Jesus died then showed up in the room where his disciples were all hiding out together.

"Rabbi, is that really you?" I imagine them asking.

"It's really me," he replied. "The life I promised you? Now it's yours. But I'm holding out for the perfect moment to give it to you and the whole world. Go to Jerusalem and wait."

But that conversation with Jesus was an estimated fifty days ago now, and the inspiration they felt on the evening of Easter Sunday has been worn down by a bunch of average, forgettable days of waiting.

On the morning of day fifty, there's Peter, sizzles of shame still occasionally popping on the frying pan of his soul. Because sure, Jesus forgave him for the whole denial thing, but here he sits with all the people who watched him fail so profoundly.

There's Mary, and I wonder if she might be battling resentment. She is, after all, surrounded by all the people that abandoned her son. All the people who ran at the first sign of suffering. She can wait, but do they really deserve to be waiting next to her?

There's James, still hopeful but also wondering if all this is for real. Did they really see Jesus, or did they see what they wanted to see? Was the experience really God, or was it some combination of emotionalism and group think? *Can I trust it? Can I trust Jesus? If not, where else can I go?*

That's what waiting does to us. And that's the Jerusalem upper room where it all was about to happen.

We often imagine the supernatural power of the Holy Spirit as something we pursue and find in a special place among enlightened, mystical people. I find that the Spirit reveals himself in the understated style that's always been God's MO—a midnight wrestling match on Jacob's return to the family estate, a burning bush on an otherwise ordinary day at Moses' office, a manger on a sleepy night in a nowhere town.

The events of Pentecost hold to the form. The church was born in an ordinary upper room in downtown Jerusalem, with the same familiar cast of characters who'd stuck together long enough to be annoyed by one another's quirks and particularities, on the fiftieth day of an otherwise underwhelming prayer meeting.

THE COMMUNITY LEFT BEHIND BY THE SPECTACLE

The day of Pentecost was something to behold—tongues of fire, expressions as raucous as drunkenness, a sermon heard in a multitude of languages simultaneously, thousands baptized. It was a spectacle. Though as powerful as it was, that wasn't what unwound the watching world. Rather, it was the community left behind by the spectacle.

The power of Pentecost was worked out in keeping with where and how it started—among ordinary communities, gathering humbly in ordinary rooms, for mostly forgettable and occasionally quite spectacular prayer and worship.

The author of Pentecost is understated, making himself known among the ordinary, seemingly preferring the company of the humble and faithful to the spiritual adrenaline junkies. The day of Pentecost was loud and public, but Pentecost kept going and keeps going quietly in the communal life of all who receive the Holy Spirit.

There is a subtle but prevalent dichotomy between the fruit of the Spirit and the gifts of the Spirit in today's church. Some communities seem taken with the long, slow work of character formation depicted in Galatians 5 as the Spirit's fruit—love, joy, peace, forbearance, kindness, goodness, faithfulness, gentleness, and self-control.[1] Other communities seem equally taken with the supernatural manifestations depicted in 1 Corinthians 12 as the Spirit's gifts, which are freely and dynamically given to and through the believer—wisdom, knowledge, faith, healing, miraculous powers, prophecy, discernment, tongues, and the interpretation of tongues.[2]

Yet the Spirit's fruit and gifts are not at odds but interconnected. Sought apart from each other, they are at best incomplete and at worst dysfunctional. The meeting point of these streams, where they flow together producing a powerful current, is community—local, rooted, often underwhelming, and ultimately transformative community.

THE TROUBLE WITH TRANSIENCE

If we are to know the ancient fruit of Pentecost in the modern church, we must learn to live deeply rooted, despite the fact that we live in a culture of transient lives and transactional relationships. These are not friendly conditions for the ancient way of deep community, so before turning to the invitation, it's important we recognize the resistance.

Transient Western culture

American journalist Sebastian Junger covered the war in Afghanistan for over a decade, living mostly in military outposts with US troops. It was there he noticed a strange phenomenon. Many soldiers voluntarily returned to the war for second, third, and fourth deployments. The soldiers he bunked next to in the barracks, who daydreamed for months about returning home to peace and ordinary life, would turn back up six months later. They'd been home briefly, then voluntarily reenlisted. Junger started to ask, "Why is it that, for so many, war seems to feel better than peace and a hard life in the barracks among comrades is preferable to a cozy life in the suburbs among friends and family?"[3]

That question led to his book *Tribe*, in which he explores a parallel phenomenon in American history: a surprising number of early American settlers, after being raised in European society and traveling across an ocean to set up that very social order in a new world, *left their society to join the Native tribes of America*. And there are next to no examples of the opposite—a native leaving the tribe to join the colonial society.

Who would willingly choose an objectively harder life—one with less comfort, convenience, and familiarity—when offered an alternative? It's the same question Sebastian Junger was asking of those soldiers he saw pining to leave the barracks then eager to return. His conclusion is that a robust sense of community and an embodied counterculture does more to draw out the human heart than comfort, wealth, ease, or social "progress" ever could.

And that's not one journalist's take from the position of hindsight. It was the consensus at the time. Connecting the dots from the seventeenth-century American frontier to the twentieth-century war-torn Middle East, Junger makes this conclusion: "A person living in a modern city or a suburb can, for the first time in history, go through an entire day—or an entire life—mostly encountering complete strangers. They can be surrounded by others and yet feel deeply, dangerously alone. The evidence that this is hard on us is overwhelming."[4] Junger's conclusion is that soldiers return to war for the same reason that European settlers returned to the woods: because they found a community in a thicker sense.

Even in the years since his book's publication, transience has continued to become ever more normalized in our culture, increasing the problem Junger diagnoses. Our societies are profoundly individualized and anticommunal, and we are bouncing from place to place, city to city, school district to school district, like never before in human history.

Shigehiro Oishi, a social psychologist at the University of Virginia, studied the effects of transience, concluding that "recent research has shown that residential mobility is associated with the primacy of the personal over the collective self."[5] He discovered that transient people pursue "duty-free relationships" and flee "obligatory relationships." They pursue "personal forms of subjective well-being" (based on self-esteem and the verification of the individualized self) and tend to discount and discard "interpersonal forms of subjective well-being" (based on social support and the building up of the community).

The ideas and motivations undergirding our transient culture are false—or at the very least, incomplete. Oishi's research exposes that the Western world has an increasingly high view of the self and celebrates autonomy . . . and an increasingly low view of community. Acted out, that idea makes us lonely, anxious, sick, and insecure—medically and psychologically speaking.

Our transient culture *resists* formation in community. And how convenient it would be to stop there, but we can't. Because the church is not, in this respect, a distinct counter-culture telling an alternative story but a reflection of the same.

Transient Western church

The common discipleship structures of the American church are built almost entirely around individualized spiritual practice while accommodating or (even worse) celebrating and assuming transience. And please don't misunderstand me: Individual spiritual practices are essential for your spiritual formation. But we are also formed through relationship. I'm talking about relationships with both those you find easy to be around and life-giving as well as with those Jesus calls your "brother and sister" but you'd be fine if they were cut out of the family will.

Community is an essential and irreplaceable part of our spiritual formation, but "rootedness" is out of style—in the culture and in the church—limiting the power of the collective to shape us.

Theologian and historian Carl Trueman notes that, for the first time in recorded history, those of us in the modern West participate in communities as autonomous individuals. Previous participation in any form of community involved the sacrifice of the self in service to the whole. The trade union, PTA, city council, and church all were participated in as a sacrifice of individuality for a greater, communal good. Today we go on participating in communities like these, but the order of our values is reversed. My participation in community is based on its service to me, and if a community stops benefiting my individual needs, I withdraw. The community serves the self. Trueman writes, "Institutions cease to be places for the formation of individuals via their schooling in the various practices and disciplines that allow them to take their place in society. Instead they become platforms for performance."[6]

The American church, often captured by the values of broader culture, has become a platform for individual performance more than an academy for discipleship to Jesus. And it doesn't take a social scientist to see that when the church becomes a stage on which a leader performs for an adoring crowd, it destroys both those in the pews and the performer on the stage. The church, stripped of the robust value of formation in community, is leaking its lifeblood.

There's nothing wrong with moving. I've done it at the same rate (or more) than the average young adult. But there are spiritual dangers to our transient culture. And if I am not aware of them, I import the values of our society into the church—exalting the individual over the group, potentially stalling my maturity by bouncing from church to church, and holding *my* spiritual journey as more important than *our* spiritual journey.

SPIRITUAL DE-FORMATION

This combination of a culture resistant to formation in community and a church swallowing that false narrative whole has led to a tragic misconception: Much of what passes as spiritual formation today, actually and ironically, *resists* spiritual formation in community. This misconception is revealed in two subtle deceptions: an individualized form of wholeness and a solitary way of spiritual devotion.

An individualized form of wholeness

We live in an increasingly therapeutic culture. The very personal formation that, for generations, was worked out in community is now being outsourced to individualized counseling and therapy. And I'm all for counseling and therapy. I've benefited from seeing a counselor myself, and I believe there is absolutely formation to be gained there. But it should be formation *in addition to* community, not *at the expense of* community.

The great psychological breakthrough of our time is that much of the deepest healing happens with a trained professional, one-on-one. We've had breakthroughs in mental health therapy that are so good and part of our redemption. On the other side of the coin, though, the great myth of our time is that we can be healed completely (or healed most deeply) in isolation—that community is not necessary to my healing or yours. The truth, affirmed by both spirituality and psychology, is that community is the context of our deepest and most complete healing.

A solitary way of spiritual devotion

Early every morning I read Scripture and pray from a chair on my porch. I also have a two-year-old. Sometimes he wakes up unusually early and interrupts my devoted time of prayer.

So here's the question: Is Amos an interruption to my prayer or is he how God is coming to me in my prayer? Can I love God by sacrificially loving my son, or only by praying in isolated solitude? Can I love God by holding Amos, fixing him breakfast, and letting his mom sleep a few extra minutes? Can I worship God by enjoying time with my son? And can God love me, satisfy me, speak to me, and fill me up through Amos?

I think so. In fact, I'd say that, for me at the moment, based on my personality and temperament, becoming more *interruptible* in my spiritual practice does more to form me into the image of Jesus than becoming more *intentional* in my spiritual practice.

We could, of course, swing too far to the other side, where our life with God becomes so others-dependent that it's unhealthy. But, by and large, this is not our danger. The opposite is the more pressing danger—relating to God through a set of spiritual practices (the way I relate to a diet or workout plan) and relating to people through some combination of mood, preference, and margin. "Many Christians would rather look into their Bibles than into the eyes of a fellow human being," writes Mike Mason. "Many will pray, 'Lord I want to be close to You,' yet never do anything to get close to the people around them. But God has designed it so that the route to Him lies through other people."[7]

Union with God that doesn't draw me nearer to others is not apprenticeship to Jesus but a distortion of it.

When asked the greatest commandment, Jesus joined two together—love for God and love for others. We meet God in personal, private, individualized spiritual practice, and we meet God in other people. Provided, of course, we go looking for the same thing in both places—union with God.

This is the litmus test of all spiritual formation: Is it leading me deeper into community or isolation? Jesus led the twelve, who would've never chosen each other for best friends, socially speaking, deeper into relationship to one another and deeper into the community with those they'd spent a lifetime avoiding. If it's Jesus we're following, we'll find ourselves going those same places.

REMAIN ROOTED

"Remain in me, as I also remain in you. No branch can bear fruit by itself; it must remain in the vine. Neither can you bear fruit unless you remain in me."[8]

"Remain." That's the repeated refrain. Jesus says that word seven times in John chapter 15 alone. In the original Greek, it's *meno*, which can be translated "remain, stay, abide."[9] John Mark Comer offers the translation, "Make your home in me as I make my home in you."[10] In context, Jesus uses this word to explain the promise of the Holy Spirit, who Jesus calls "another Advocate to help you and be with you forever" later in the passage. On his final night, Jesus promised his faithful followers, "My very Spirit will make its home in you just as you've seen in me, making your life radiant like mine." The participatory invitation, the way Jesus invites us to join the Spirit's inner transformation, is simple and straightforward. Remain. Abide. Stay. *Meno.*

While there is certainly an abstract, mystical component to this, we should not ignore the concrete and grounded expression— root your life in a community of Jesus' followers. The fruit and the gifts, character formation and supernatural manifestations, all of these grow in the soil of deeply rooted community.

Among the ancient, preserved wisdom of the Christian desert fathers and mothers you'll find, "Just as a tree cannot bear fruit if it is often transplanted, so neither can a monk bear fruit if he frequently changes his abode."[11] This is an idea borrowed from Paul's letter to the Galatians: "But the fruit of the Spirit is love, joy, peace, forbearance, kindness, goodness, faithfulness, gentleness and self-control."[12]

The most famous and popularized version of this desert wisdom came through Saint Benedict, who authored the Benedictine Rule, a set of commitments to order the life of an emerging group of monks. Monastic orders like this were popping up all over during his time. What was unique about Benedict's Rule is its very first commitment, which was entirely original and found in no other monastic writing of its time: a vow of stability—a radical commitment to live a rooted life, in a fixed place, among an imperfect people. It was a vow to take the good with the bad in one community over the long haul.

Why a vow of stability? Because Benedict's time apparently wasn't all that different from our own. He was observing all the ways instability and a spirituality of "self over community" was stunting maturity. He writes of a group of monks he names *gyrovagues*, a combination of two Latin words, *gyro* meaning "circle" and *vagues* meaning "wander." Gyrovagues were those "wandering in circles."[13] They were "rootless" followers of Jesus. Saint Benedict comments, "Always on the move, they never settle down, and are slaves to their own wills and gross appetites."[14]

The modern-day gyrovague is the sincerely committed Jesus follower who finds himself or herself bouncing from church to church. The vow of stability isn't a critique of transience. It's a pathway to spiritual maturity.

The fruit of the Spirit is not grown abstractly. You and I must be deeply rooted to bear fruit. We grow in patience by bearing with difficult people when running would be much easier. We grow goodness by remaining in relationship with people through conflict. Self-control grows in soil where we're tempted toward outbursts of gossip or anger. Spiritual maturity is relational and particular.

The way of Jesus essentially involves relationship because without community, there is no way for us to grow to become more like Jesus. The way of Jesus is particular to a place because the

Kingdom of God is not an abstract utopia we ascend to but an invading reality coming to every square inch of earth.

The Kingdom comes when I turn the other cheek, which presupposes brothers, sisters, and neighbors who occasionally wrong me. The Kingdom comes when I grow quick to listen and slow to speak, which assumes there are perspectives of others I'll want to talk over or run from but will be refined by listening empathetically to. The Kingdom comes when I seek the prosperity of the city, meaning the city in which I follow Jesus isn't prospering according to His design already.

In his brilliant book *When the Church Was a Family*, Joseph Hellerman writes,

> Spiritual formation occurs primarily in the context of community. People who remain connected with their brothers and sisters in the local church almost invariably grow in self-understanding, and they mature in their ability to relate in healthy ways to God and to their fellow human beings. This is especially the case for those courageous Christians who stick it out through the often messy process of interpersonal discord and conflict resolution. Long-term interpersonal relationships are the crucible of genuine progress in the Christian life. People who stay also grow.[15]

He goes on to admit the immediate gratification of the alternative—that running will provide immediate relief from the awkwardness or pain of remaining, but you're destined to find yourself in this exact spot in the next community. Because, in the simple and humbling words of monastic author Thomas à Kempis: "Wherever you go, there you are!"[16]

A healthy church community, stuck with through disillusionment and stuck with over a long period of time, is an anchor and a filter—an anchor that holds me in God's presence, and a filter that purifies my character from the inside out.

The Big Book of Alcoholics Anonymous expresses the same concept. The founders of AA discovered that a personal formation problem (like alcoholism) could be overcome only by spiritual experience. And the context where that all gets worked out? Regular meetings in large community and deep relationship with a sponsor. Spirituality is inherently relational. My deepest transformation requires the intervening rescue of God. And my deepest transformation is fostered in community.

Are there good reasons to leave? Of course. Are there toxic and unhealthy churches where staying stunts growth and leaving promotes it? Absolutely. I'm simply noting that, on the whole, we short-circuit our spiritual formation by wandering, not by staying.

What if the greatest obstacle to our formation isn't, in fact, culture clashes, ideological division, technology hijacking our brains, or wealth stealing our affection? What if our greatest obstacle is the one the culture and the church jointly celebrate: wanderlust?

We are a future-oriented society addicted to the next and the new. The grass is always greener, and we are forever living in the desire for some day other than now and some place other than here. We tinker with our lives through our circumstances, assuming that the character beneath those circumstances will become new if we change the scenery. We try to form character by running from one set of circumstances to another. But Jesus says character is shaped when we abide, remain, stay, *meno*. When we surrender to our here and now, accepting the blessings and limitations they offer, the Spirit of the living God forms us into Jesus' image.

POWER FLOWS THROUGH LOVE

As Pentecost continued to get worked out in the early church, we eventually reach 1 Corinthians 14, a manifesto on the proper exercise of the gifts of the Spirit in the gathered community. A chapter which, in between all the talk of signs and wonders, includes the oft-overlooked command, "Since you are eager for manifestations of the Spirit, strive to excel in building up the church."[17]

In the early church they never imitated the miracles of Jesus without equally imitating the love of Jesus. They moved toward pain, toward hurts and annoyances and grievances, toward the need in one another. They learned to forgive and ask forgiveness. They saw the worst in each other and kept choosing love. Power always serves love—never the other way around. The Bible calls power apart from love a noisy gong and a clanging cymbal.[18]

Are you eager for manifestations of the Spirit? Are you longing for signs and wonders? For supernatural physical healing and deep inner healing? For the ground-shaking word of prophecy and the still small whisper to the soul? For the fiery power of intercession and the society-altering justice that follows? Then channel all your energy into loving those in your local church who you find are the hardest to love.

Do you want the power of the Spirit? Listen to one another. Ask good, thoughtful questions, and then really listen. Be patient with one another. Have time for each other. Invite someone else in. Discomfort yourself to expand your friend group, to share your lunch plans, to open up your home.

Are you eager for manifestations of the Spirit? Then make your ambition the slow, subtle, intentional gift of loving one another.

William J. Seymour, leader of the Azusa Street Revival in Los Angeles in the early 1900s and founder of the Pentecostal tradition, wrote, "The Pentecostal power, when you sum it all up, is just more of God's love. If it does not bring more of God's love, it is simply a counterfeit. Pentecost means to live right in the thirteenth chapter of First Corinthians, which is the standard."[19]

Let me remind you of something you know but tend to forget: Life is about relationship. On your deathbed, you will not be thinking about accomplishments or failures, what you got done or left undone. You will not be proudly or shamefully scanning your resume or bank account. You will not be crossing off your to-do list. When the lights are going out on your numbered days this side of eternity, you will not be thinking about whatever's stressing you today. You'll be thinking about people. The people you got to spend your life with. How you loved them or didn't. How you prioritized them or didn't. What you sacrificed to know them more deeply or what got in the way.

What I'm trying to make absolutely plain to you, friends, is that the spectacle of Pentecost came in tongues of fire and rushing wind, but the sustaining power of Pentecost came in a community of people humbly and stubbornly loving one another. If it's the power of Pentecost we're after, we'd do well to look as much to the people on our right and left as we do up to the heavens.

The gift of the Holy Spirit means signs, wonders, and miracles. And the greatest miracle of all just might be living in a community of love over the long haul.

LOOKING AT ONE PLACE DEEPLY

Larry McMurtry became a household name for his epic novel *Lonesome Dove*. But I've been moved by another, much less acclaimed work—a memoir of sorts about all the roads he's traveled across the US. The places his work has taken him, people he's met, and all he's seen. It's a sweeping adventure story that makes you want to live on the road, to set out on a great adventure, a celebration of wanderlust.

But he ends back where his story began—in the small east Texas town he was born in, thinking of his father, who rarely ventured past the dusty dirt roads of that little town. Holding his life up next to his father's, McMurtry writes, "I have looked at many places quickly. My father looked at one place deeply."[20]

These days we tend to confuse depth with breadth. If I've traveled a lot, seen a lot of people, looked at a lot of places, I'm "cultured." And that's respected. And, honestly, I think it should be. I believe there's an opportunity for depth via interaction with many different people, places, and ways of thought. But what we fail to see is that there is equally an opportunity for depth in simple stability.

The apostle Paul traveled the major cities of the Greco-Roman world on a missional adventure for the ages, a page-turning epic of people groups and cultures, floggings and shipwrecks, painful goodbyes and world-changing sermons.

Jesus, the one whose story Paul took on the road, lived less like Paul, less like me, and more like my grandmother Evelyn. Deeply rooted. Jesus was known by many, traveled from town to town, and gave his life for all of us. But he gave himself deeply to just a few, embracing the limitations of humanity's relational capacity and numbered days. Jesus cultivated depth in simple stability, and I wonder if we've lost a taste for that.

I wonder what treasures we're forfeiting in the name of wanderlust. I wonder if there might be some among us who dig deep enough, for long enough, in one place among one people, to uncover those ancient treasures again.

To root yourself deeply—among a people and a place over the long haul—there lies a great opportunity for depth.

PRACTICE: COMMUNITY

Jesus' twelve closest disciples relationally bridged the socioeconomic, ideological, and political lines of ancient Israel. Blue-collar workers, tax collectors, and Zealots all right there together. You've got tribal tension, vocational tension, class tension, political tension, social tension, and we're just talking about the twelve here—the inner ring. It's beautiful to reflect on the compelling outcome of that sort of intentional diversity, but for the individuals Jesus called, they had to work through real discomfort and tension to follow him.

The early church that grew from the apostles included this paradox—a compelling, redemptive stick of dynamite in the social architecture of the ancient world, and an absolute mess of relational tension, conflict, and division that needed mending. They were a hospitable, loving, generous, sacrificial, revolutionary family, and the day-in, day-out experience in that family included conflict, segregation, incest, false teaching, cultural colonization, and ignoring the poor, among other issues. It was a mess—a lively, compelling mess, but don't mistake it for anything but a mess. Eugene Peterson concluded simply, "There are no 'successful' congregations in Scripture."[21]

Given the messiness of church communities, perhaps we shouldn't be surprised that there's a growing sentiment that goes something like "I'm into Jesus but not the church."

First, I should say that much of the felt experience behind that statement can be completely legitimate. Historically and recently some (but not all) Christian churches have been guilty of financial corruption, racism, manipulation, abuse of every variety, and ego-driven, self-centered Kingdom building. That's tragic viewed on a large scale, but of course the real tragedy is the individuals for whom the family of God has been a wounding family rather than a healing one. And if that's your story, I'm genuinely so, so sorry. That's not the heart of the Rabbi we follow or the heart of the church.

Second, I want to say clearly that the major problem with "I'm into Jesus and not the church" is Jesus. If you're really into Jesus, you *know* that the church was never optional in his mind. Jesus was not anti-institutional. He regularly led his followers into the two religious institutions of first-century Judea: the synagogue and the temple. And those institutions' faults are well documented on the pages of Scripture. Despite his own legitimate criticism of the "church" of his day, Jesus did not abandon it. He kept showing up, kept praying with the people in the pews, kept receiving the Word in the context of brothers and sisters.

Following Jesus means following him into communities of healing that are also riddled with the disease. If you're looking for a solitary, "me, my journal, and an ambient Icelandic playlist in my earbuds" version of following Jesus, you won't find it on the pages of Scripture.

All to say, the proper context for the presence and power of the Holy Spirit, manifested through common gifts and expressions like discernment, prophecy, healing, witness, and redemptive suffering, is the local church. If you are eager to grow in the power of the Holy Spirit, commit yourself to community. Find a local church—a shopping mall–sized megachurch; a centuries-old, liturgically rooted congregation; a humble house church in a living room; or something in between. Commit yourself to a local gathering of Jesus followers you will know and be known by, comfort and grieve among, confess to and receive confession from. Commit yourself to a community where power flows through love.

EPILOGUE

THE ONE CALLED
ALONGSIDE TO HELP

And I will ask the Father, and he will give you another advocate to help you and be with you forever—the Spirit of truth. The world cannot accept him, because it neither sees him nor knows him. But you know him, for he lives with you and will be in you.

JOHN 14:16–17

"TYLER, THE DOCTOR JUST CALLED," Kirsten sounded frantic. "There's something wrong with the baby's heart."

I was in the basement of an old Ethiopian church in central London, helping to lead the final worship gathering on a week-long whirlwind tour through the UK. Kirsten is the strongest and most independent person I know. I could count on one hand the number of times she'd called me consecutively, so when my phone buzzed with her name for the second time, I feared something was wrong.

I flew halfway around the world first thing the following

morning, finally landing back home in Portland. Within twenty-four hours we were sitting together in the doctor's office as they performed an ultrasound for more than an hour, not saying a word. The silence was eerie, as if everyone else knew something—something that would devastate us—but no one wanted to be the one to have to say it out loud.

Our youngest son, Amos, was diagnosed with a heart condition seven months out from the delivery date. Not just any heart condition but the most severe heart condition a developing infant can potentially survive. The tricky aspect of the diagnosis is that it has to do with the way the heart filters oxygen in the blood, meaning the infant develops healthily in the womb, but at the moment of birth, when the baby breathes oxygen for the first time, a clock starts ticking fast. Survival is a coin flip, and even those children who do survive are often seriously impaired, physically or cognitively or both.

The doctor explained all this to us, instructing us to prepare for the worst—likely loss of life within the first few days after birth. I was in shock, not able to properly process the news. Kirsten was composed but silent throughout the appointment. I asked the questions. She just sat there, taking it in.

We walked back through the waiting room, scheduling the first of what was suddenly many necessary follow-up appointments, and then the elevator doors closed. At that very moment, the two of us alone in the privacy of a steel box for a few seconds, Kirsten erupted in a wail like I've never heard before or since. She wept in agonizing screams I'll never forget and didn't stop for hours.

When we got home I relieved the babysitter. Took Hank and Simon, our older two boys, to the playground in an attempt to shield them from seeing their mother in such grief. Maybe, in hindsight, I was trying to shield myself from feeling what she felt.

Kirsten never came out of our bedroom that night.

I made boxed mac and cheese for dinner, brushed the boys' little teeth, tucked them into bed, and then I had to face it—had to be alone, with no one to comfort, nothing to busy myself with, no help to serve as a distraction from what I didn't know how to face.

ONE CALLED ALONGSIDE TO HELP

In Jesus' lengthy final conversation with his disciples, to which we keep returning, the most frequent name he gives to the Holy Spirit is the Greek *parakletos*. This title is rightly summarized in the English as "advocate" (as the NIV translates it) or "helper" (as some other reputable translations opt for), but is most fully and literally translated "one called alongside to help."

Jesus calls the Holy Spirit by three revealing names: Comforter, Advocate, and Counselor. In the long and unpredictable race of the spiritual life, we've been given a Comforter to draw near, never leaving us alone in our pain; an Advocate to defend us against the harassing constancy of the deceiver's lies; a Counselor to listen, prodding us along with pointed questions, aiding us in interpreting the complex plot points of our individual stories into puzzle pieces that fit coherently into the whole.

Comforter

Talking with his disciples on the evening of his arrest, Jesus' first reference to the Holy Spirit is followed by a promise: "I will not leave you as orphans; I will come to you."[1] This promise has a three-part meaning. Jesus will come and find his disciples in the inevitable chaos that will envelop them following his arrest and crucifixion. Jesus is also pointing forward, to his promised return to establish the full effects of the victory he will accomplish through his sacrifice. But most presently, this promise is connected to the promise that precedes it—the gift of the Holy Spirit, who is the felt experiential presence of God and will never leave us nor forsake us.

Life in this world is unpredictable. Desperation pounces on

us, wrestles us to the ground. The power of God's intervention is promised to every one of his children, but the expression of that intervention is mysterious. Even when God does not come in might, he comes in comfort. He will not leave us as orphans. And those who know the Comforter, particularly amid desperation, discover the quiet but mighty truth: The presence of God is more powerful than my pain. His comfort outlasts my desperation and even makes a way through it.

Advocate

The Holy Spirit, according to Jesus, is our advocate, pleading our case, even when we don't have the words to speak. Romans 8 assures us that the Spirit intercedes for us, meaning the Spirit speaks up on our behalf, in groans too deep for words. In life's desperate moments, we often struggle to find the words. We don't know what to ask for or how to say it, or maybe the circumstances are so dark that we've lost the will even to pray. And in that place, for that place, we are promised an ever-present Advocate.

The most common biblical name given to our spiritual enemy is "accuser." We have a deceiver constantly harassing us with lies that, like the original lie that infected the whole world, seek to minimize our view of self and chip away at our trust in God.

And it's for that very reason that I find such significance in the fact that Jesus names the Spirit "Advocate." It's the exact opposite. The Spirit is the antidote to our opposition. The accuser seeks to isolate us, driving us away from God, and the Spirit nudges and prods us back in God's direction, assuring us that everywhere we turn we are in his loving gaze. The Spirit assures us of our untakable, unlosable belovedness.

The Holy Spirit convicts the world. Jesus is perfectly clear about that. But the Spirit advocates for those who belong to God, incessantly assuring you of your identity with a still, small voice that whispers, "Beloved. Beloved. Beloved."

The Spirit convicts the world so that all who belong to this world might turn and become family. But to the adopted, the Spirit reminds us that we *are* family. Returning to Romans 8, we discover that the Holy Spirit living within all of Christ's followers cries out from within our chests, "Abba, Father!"

Counselor

If you've ever been to counseling, you'll know that you go in with a "presenting issue." You enlist a counselor to help you solve an internal puzzle you can't seem to piece together—your bouts of rage toward your children, emotional unavailability toward your spouse, or over-attachment to your career. You go in with a "presenting issue," but that's never why you're really there. The skilled counselor works like a surgeon, only instead of a scalpel she cuts you open with innocent-but-pointed questions until she finds that one that unravels you. That's when you find out that, while your presenting issue may have gotten you here, it's not why you're really here. You're actually here in search of healing from a wound inflicted in childhood you've never stopped bleeding from, a false identity you medicate with a subtle but addicted behavior pattern, a loss you buried and forgot that has grown like a seed of resentment overtaking your person.

In the first-century Mediterranean world where Jesus lived his thirty-three years, people weren't just aware of wind. They relied on wind. For Jesus and his companions, the wind wasn't just a noticeable or ignorable breeze that sang in the trees; it was the resource they relied on for transportation the way the modern world relies on fuel.

In one gospel scene Jesus slumbered in the bow of the boat while his disciples fought for their lives against the raging storm. When Jesus woke and calmed the storm, the relieved passengers exclaimed, "What kind of man is this? Even the wind and the waves obey him!"[2] Later Peter, one of those on the boat that day, referred to the biblical prophets as those "carried along by the Holy Spirit."[3] It all evokes the image of the wind not rustling the leaves of summer trees but propelling a boat in a direction—sailing. *Parakletos*, "one called alongside to help"—that's the title Jesus gave the Holy Spirit on that final night, repeated four times in a single conversation. It's a title with ancient maritime roots.

In the first-century Greco-Roman world, if you were out fishing in the Mediterranean and got lost at sea somewhere between Santorini and Mykonos, your only hope would be a *parakletos*. This was the common term for a rescue boat, which would attach to yours and tow you back into the harbor. That boat, the *parakletos*, would "draw alongside to help," bringing you safely home.

Who is the Holy Spirit? The one called alongside to help. The one who comes and finds you when you're lost and alone, and pulls you back to the heart of the Father.

HOLY SPIRIT, COME AND FIND ME

So there I am: alone and undistracted in the paralyzing uncertainty of Amos's diagnosis. We've got a baby coming in seven months—little Amos, who may grace us with his presence for decades, days, or merely hours; Amos, whose life may be so impaired he will never ride a bike next to his brothers, write his name at the top of a kindergarten worksheet, or move out and into his first grimy apartment downtown. He could be one of the lucky ones, sure, but the doctors prepared us for the worst. Told us to practice saying goodbye. How do you practice saying goodbye to someone you won't say hello to for seven more months?

I'm sure I did sleep in spurts that night, but I don't remember dozing off for even a minute. Finally, at 4:00 a.m., I got up. I didn't know what else to do, only that I didn't want to be at home. Couldn't sit still. I went for a run in the pitch-black night.

After wandering the dark streets of Portland like a mad man for who knows how many miles, I sat down, physically, emotionally, and spiritually exhausted by the weight of it all. I sat on my front porch—the holy ground place I pray every morning—and in the dark and cold of that late-autumn morning, I finally got a word out. I voiced a response to the Great Counselor I'd gone twelve rounds with over the course of a sleepless night, a prayer to verbalize the Spirit's groaning that hadn't quieted in my soul since I picked up that phone call in the basement of the Ethiopian church in central London.

"Holy Spirit, come and find me," I prayed aloud. "I'm lost. Can't find land. Holy Spirit, come and find me. Draw me back to harbor, back to the heart of the Father. I need the *parakletos*."

When I said his name—Counselor—I unraveled. A dam broke behind my tear ducts and I didn't weep; I wailed. I wailed alone on the front porch like Kirsten had in that hospital elevator. It was the first of many such sessions with the Counselor as I rode out the next two hundred days of desperation, awaiting Amos's birth.

We all come in with a presenting issue, right? Every client in every counselor's waiting room. Every disciple who knows the great Counselor. And he, like a master therapist, does not do his work with quick answers because, of course, quick answers might comfort for a moment but they won't heal. The Counselor asks questions that unravel us because only those unraveling kinds of questions can lead us into true healing.

At the time I'm writing this epilogue, Amos is healthy, twenty months old, and the happiest, smiliest little guy you've ever met. He's had three open-heart surgeries, and his journey is far from over. But he plays with his brothers and has no apparent cognitive or physical limitations from his condition. Our story thus far has ended not in grief but in joy, and "grateful" is far too small a word for that.

But when I see that smile on his little round face, I remember the Holy Spirit. The Comforter who strengthened me daily for two hundred days like he fed the Israelites manna. The Advocate who exposed the many lies that harassed every step of the journey. The Counselor who took my appointments every day but started by drawing alongside to help, tugging me back to harbor.

ACKNOWLEDGMENTS

THANK YOU to Andrew Stoddard, Daniel Marrs, Natalie Nyquist, and the entire team at Thomas Nelson who honed this book from the rambles of my typing fingers into a coherent offering. Every step of the way, you've been a joy to work alongside.

Thank you to my literary agent Austin Wilson, my creative director Katya Wawrykow, and (most especially) my unreasonably competent and astoundingly kind executive assistant Jenny DeKorte, all of whom have worked tirelessly to see this book from idea in my head to paper in your hands. I am deeply grateful for each of your unique support—in both my work and personhood.

A massive thanks is owed to my very generous friends Tim Mackie, Aaron Shaw, John Mark Comer, Gemma Ryan, and Gerry Breshears, all of whom worked with the very earliest manuscripts of this book to offer encouragement, correction, and (much needed) edits—acts of sacrificial love with their very valuable time and attention.

Thank you to Bridgetown Church, among whom this book's contents have been both taught and practiced, worked from a living invitation on the pages of Scripture into real-life stories and practices in community.

Thank you, more than anyone, to my family: Hank, this book is for you, and my prayer is that its message lives in you far more than it ever has or will in me. Simon, I adore you—every bit of you—just as you are. Never change. With God's help, may you grow more fully into your true self every day. Amos, you bring me more joy than any human on the planet. Less screaming would be welcome, but stay wild, no matter the cost. Kirsten, you are my best friend, the most beautiful person I've ever seen and known, and the one whose voice I'll never tire of listening to. I love you. Thank you for putting up with my ridiculous idiosyncrasies, for listening to me verbally process this book's pieces (and so many other topics), and for celebrating each step of it coming to life with me. Writing is a bear. This book has been no exception. Let's all take a break, go somewhere fun, laugh together, and make some new memories before attempting this again. We've earned it—all of us.

NOTES

Introduction
1. Ephesians 3:10.
2. Dr. Michael Glock, "Individuation in Jungian Psychology: Unraveling the Fragmented Self," *Medium*, January 11, 2024, https://medium.com/@drmichaelglock/individuation-in-jungian-psychology-unraveling-the-fragmented-self-06eb2eda02d4.
3. Acts 19:2.

Part 1: When the Advocate Comes
1. Marjorie Thompson, *Soul Feast: An Invitation to the Christian Spiritual Life, Newly Revised Edition* (Westminster John Knox Press, 2014), xix.

Chapter 1: The Familiar Stranger
1. John 16:7.
2. Kevin P. Emmert, "New Poll Finds Evangelicals' Favorite Heresies," *Christianity Today*, October 28, 2014, https://www.christianitytoday.com/ct/2014/october-web-only/new-poll-finds-evangelicals-favorite-heresies.html.
3. Ligonier Ministries, "The State of Theology," https://thestateoftheology.com/, quoted in Stefani McDade, "Top 5 Heresies Among American Evangelicals," *Christianity Today*, September 19, 2022, https://www.christianitytoday.com/ct/2022/september-web-only/state-of-theology-evangelical-heresy-report-ligonier-survey.html.

4. Genesis 1:1–2.

5. Strong's Hebrew, "7307.ruach," Bible Hub, accessed June 20, 2024, https://biblehub.com/hebrew/7307.htm; Strong's Greek, "4151.pneuma," Bible Hub, accessed June 20, 2024, https://bible hub.com/greek/4151.htm.

6. Genesis 2:7.

7. See Genesis 2:7; 6:17.

8. Isaiah 33:20.

9. Exodus. 40:34.

10. 1 Kings 8:10–11.

11. Exodus 19:12–13.

12. John 1:14.

13. John 2:19.

14. John 2:21.

15. John 20:22–23.

16. 1 Corinthians 3:16.

17. 1 Corinthians 6:19–20.

18. John 14:12.

19. Eugene Peterson, *The Pastor: A Memoir* (HarperOne, 2011), 214.

20. Billy Graham, "How to Be Filled with the Spirit," sermon, Greater Los Angeles Crusade, 1949.

21. Acts 1:1.

22. Simon Ponsonby, *More: How You Can Have More of the Spirit When You Already Have Everything in Christ* (David C. Cook, 2010), 29.

23. Curt Thompson, *Anatomy of the Soul: Surprising Connections Between Neuroscience and Spiritual Practices That Can Transform Your Life and Relationships* (Tyndale Refresh, 2010), 16.

24. See Exodus 34:14.

Chapter 2: Breath

1. Genesis 1:28.

2. Isaiah 65:17–18.

3. Eugene Peterson, *Christ Plays in Ten Thousand Places: A Conversation in Spiritual Theology* (Eerdmans, 2008), 22.

4. Ezekiel 37:3, 9–10.

5. Matthew 3:17.

6. Mark 1:22.
7. Genesis 1:3.
8. John 20:22.
9. Acts 2:1–4.
10. Acts 2:4.
11. 2 Corinthians 4:7.
12. John 14:25–26.
13. John 16:13, 15 ESV.
14. Psalm 103:11.
15. Psalm 103:12.
16. Romans 5:5.
17. Genesis 4:1 ESV.
18. Brennan Manning, *Abba's Child: The Cry of the Heart for Intimate Belonging* (NavPress, 2015), 39.

Chapter 3: Water

1. Genesis 1:1–2.
2. In the Bible "the waters" can be used as a symbol of chaos and disorder (like the ocean waters or the flood) or as a sign of God's gift of life, when the waters are channeled into a river or when they spring up from a well. For more background on the multiple meanings of water in the Bible, check out this helpful episode from the BibleProject podcast: "One Creation Story or Two? Ancient Cosmology Series: Episode 4," June 7, 2021 on *BibleProject*, produced by Dan Grummel, Zach McKinley, and Cooper Pelz, MP3 audio, 41:00, https://bibleproject.com/podcast/one-creation-story-or-two/.
3. See Job and Psalms 74 and 89; also the thematic elements in the biblical portrayal of Egyptian and Philistine oppressors.
4. Genesis 2:10.
5. Ezekiel 47:6–12.
6. David Benner, *Surrender to Love: Discovering the Heart of Christian Spirituality* (InterVarsity Press, 2015), 61.
7. John 7:37.
8. John 7:37–38.
9. Matthew 4:19; Mark 1:17.
10. John 7:39.

11. Acts 2:33.
12. Revelation 21:1.
13. Revelation 22:1–2.
14. John 16:15.
15. John 7:38.
16. 1 Corinthians 6:19.
17. Henri Nouwen, *The Wounded Healer: Ministry in Contemporary Society* (1972; repr., Random House, 2013), 89.
18. Acts 4:13.
19. Brennan Manning, *Ruthless Trust: The Ragamuffin's Path to God* (HarperCollins, 2009), 48.
20. Isaiah 53:5.

Chapter 4: Dove

1. John 14:12.
2. Matthew 3:16; Mark 1:10; Luke 3:22; John 1:32.
3. Genesis 1:1–2.
4. Deuteronomy 32:11.
5. *Strong's Exhaustive Concordence*, s.v. "7363. rachaph," Bible Hub, accessed July 17, 2024, https://biblehub.com/hebrew/7363.htm.
6. Luke 4:18–19.
7. Luke 4:21.
8. Luke 4:1–2, 14, 16–18.
9. See chapter 2 of N. T. Wright's *How God Became King: The Forgotten Story of the Gospels* (HarperOne, 2016) for a more comprehensive sketch of the popular cultural emergence of this view and the reactive response within the Western church.
10. Acts 2:43.
11. Acts 19:12.
12. Acts 10:37–38.
13. Acts 1:1.
14. Eugene Peterson, *Practice Resurrection: A Conversation on Growing Up in Christ* (Eerdmans, 2010), 25.
15. Acts 2:43; 4:33–34; 5:12.
16. Michael Green, *I Believe in the Holy Spirit* (Eerdmans, 1975, 2004), 298.
17. Acts 4:13.

18. Parker J. Palmer, *A Hidden Wholeness: The Journey Toward an Undivided Life* (Jossey-Bass, 2009), 90.
19. John 14:12.
20. 1 John 2:20.
21. Simon Ponsonby, *More: How You Can Have More of the Spirit When You Already Have Everything in Christ* (David C Cook, 2010), 16–17.
22. A. W. Tozer, *God's Pursuit of Man* (Moody Publishers, 2015), 24.
23. Samuel Chadwick, *The Way to Pentecost* (Hodder and Stoughton, 1939), 15.
24. David Brooks, *The Second Mountain: The Quest for a Moral Life* (Random House, 2019), 114.

Chapter 5: The Curious Case of Simon the Sorcerer

1. *Merriam Webster's Collegiate Dictionary*, s.v. "trauma," accessed June 24, 2024, https://unabridged.merriam-webster.com/collegiate /trauma.
2. Resmaa Menakem, *My Grandmother's Hands: Racialized Trauma and the Pathway to Mending Our Hearts and Bodies* (Central Recovery Press, 2017), 8.
3. Rich Villodas, *Good and Beautiful and Kind: Becoming Whole in a Fractured World* (Waterbrook, 2022), 54.
4. Acts 8:5–8.
5. Acts 8:9.
6. Johann Hari, *Stolen Focus: Why You Can't Pay Attention—and How to Think Deeply Again* (Crown, 2022), 53.
7. Jeffrey Schwartz and Rebecca Gladding, *You Are Not Your Brain: The Four-Step Solution for Changing Bad Habits, Ending Unhealthy Thinking, and Taking Control of Your Life* (Penguin Publishing Group, 2011), chap. 15.
8. Mary Oliver, *Upstream: Selected Essays* (Penguin Publishing Group 2019), 8.
9. 2 Corinthians 3:17.
10. Hari, *Stolen Focus*, 54.
11. Mihaly Csikszentmihalyi, *Flow: The Psychology of Optimal Experience* (Harper Perennial Modern Classics, 2008).

Chapter 6: The Subtle Tragedy of Nicodemus

1. John 3:2.
2. John 3:3.
3. Eugene Peterson, *Christ Plays in Ten Thousand Places: A Conversation in Spiritual Theology* (CMBC Publications, 1999), 16.
4. George R. Beasley-Murray, *John*, 2nd ed., vol. 36 of Word Biblical Commentary (Word, 1999), Logos Research Edition, https://www.logos.com/product/1339/john-2nd-ed.
5. John 3:9.
6. John 7:37–39.
7. John 7:50–51.
8. John 19:38–40.
9. Nicodemus is mentioned in the Jewish Talmud, and many commentators believe his burial arrangements are extravagant, indicating that he became a revered disciple of Jesus. I certainly hope he did!
10. Michelle Obama, *Becoming* (Crown, 2018), 16.
11. Jason P. Roberts, "Conceptual Blending, the Second Naïveté, and the Emergence of New Meanings," *Open Theology* 4, no. 1 (2018): 29–45, https://doi.org/10.1515/opth-2018-0003.
12. 1 Corinthians 14:1.

Part 3: Clothed with Power from on High

1. Ed D. Pytches, "Remembering John Wimber," Vineyard USA, accessed June 24, 2024, https://vineyardusa.org/remembering-john-wimber/.
2. Ephesians 4:12.

Chapter 7: Discernment

1. Joannes Cassianus, *Collationes*, archived at University of Zurich, *Corpus Corporum*, last updated January 6, 2024, https://mlat.uzh.ch/browser/7530.
2. Thomas Green, *Weeds Among the Wheat: Discernment: Where Prayer & Action Meet* (Ave Maria Press, 1984), 21.
3. Luke 24:28.
4. 1 Kings 19:11–13.
5. 1 Kings 19:11.

6. Exodus 33:21–22.

7. Mark 6:48.

8. Luke 24:29.

9. Luke 24:32.

10. Pete Greig, *How to Hear God: A Simple Guide for Normal People* (Zondervan, 2022), 150.

11. 1 John 4:1

12. 2 Corinthians 11:14; Revelation 13:15 (see footnote in Green, *Weeds Among the Wheat,* 157).

13. Saint Ignatius, *Spiritual Exercises of St. Ignatius,* s.v. "332.4," trans. Louis J. Puhl (1951, repr., Martino Fine Books, 2010), 148.

14. Ruth Haley Barton, *Pursuing God's Will Together: A Discernment Practice of Leadership Groups* (IVP, 2012), 10.

15. Jared Patrick Boyd, *Finding Freedom in Constraint: Reimagining Spiritual Disciplines as a Communal Way of Life* (IVP, 2023), 229.

16. Genesis 2:18.

17. 1 Kings 17:2–4.

18. 1 Kings 17:7.

19. 1 Kings 17:8–9.

20. Dr. J. Robert Clinton, *The Making of a Leader: Recognizing the Lessons and Stages of Leadership Development,* 2nd ed. (NavPress, 2012).

Chapter 8: Prophecy

1. Numbers 11:25.

2. Numbers 11:29.

3. John 1:14.

4. John 20:22.

5. Joel 2:28–29.

6. 1 Corinthians 14:1, 3.

7. 1 Corinthians 14:5.

8. Dallas Willard, *Hearing God: Developing a Conversational Relationship with God* (IVP, 2012), Kindle location 995.

9. John 10:4.

10. David Fritch, *Enthroned: Bringing God's Kingdom to Earth Through Unceasing Worship & Prayer* (self-published, 2017), 94.

11. Green, *Weeds Among the Wheat*.
12. 1 Corinthians 14:1.
13. Greig, *How to Hear God*, 114.
14. Greig, 114.
15. My paraphrase from George Bernard Shaw, *Saint Joan* (1924), scene 1, archived at Project Gutenberg Australia, last modified October 2002, https://gutenberg.net.au/ebooks02/0200811h.html.
16. 1 Corinthians 13:9.
17. Greig, *How to Hear God*, 124.
18. 1 Corinthians 14:3.
19. 1 Corinthians 13:1.
20. 1 Corinthians 14:1.
21. 1 Corinthians 14:29.

Chapter 9: Healing

1. John 5:25, 28–29.
2. Dallas Willard, *The Spirit of the Disciplines: Understanding How God Changes Lives* (HarperCollins, 2009), 36.
3. 1 Corinthians 15:19.
4. Jordan Seng, *Miracle Work: A Down-to-Earth Guide to Supernatural Ministries* (IVP, 2012), 80–81.
5. Albert Haase, *Living the Lord's Prayer: The Way of the Disciple* (IVP, 2010), 160.
6. Mark 6:5–6. Matthew 10:52 records another instance of human faith being named as an ingredient to divine healing.
7. Mark 10:52.
8. See Exodus 34:6.
9. Mark 9:29.
10. Seng, *Miracle Work*, 81.
11. Matthew 6:7–8.
12. Mark 1:41.
13. Luke 7:14.
14. Matthew 9:6.
15. Acts 3:6.
16. I'm paraphrasing a talk Wimber gave; you can find a similar account in his book *Living with Uncertainty*, quoted at John Wimber, "View from the Valley," Vineyard Churches, August 8,

2012, https://www.vineyardchurches.org.uk/resources/view-from
-the-valley/.

17. Isaiah 53:5.

18. Kenneth Leech, *True Prayer: An Introduction to Christian
Spirituality* (Sheldon Press, 1980).

Chapter 10: Witness

1. James Finley, *Merton's Palace of Nowhere* (Ave Maria Press, 2003).
2. Matthew 28:18–20.
3. Luke 24:49.
4. Acts 1:4.
5. Acts 1:6.
6. Michael Green, *I Believe in the Holy Spirit: Biblical Teaching for
the Church Today* (1975; repr., Wm. B. Eerdmans, 2023), 2.
7. N. T. Wright, *Simply Jesus: A New Vision of Who He Was, What
He Did, and Why He Matters* (HarperOne, 2011), 214.
8. See John Mark Comer's brilliant book *Practicing the Way* for a
fuller treatment of this topic.
9. Alan Jones, *Soul Making: The Desert Way of Spirituality* (1970;
repr., SanFran, 1989), 161.
10. Acts 10:37–38.
11. Jürgen Moltmann, *The Way of Jesus Christ* (Minneapolis, 1993),
98–99.
12. Quoted in Mark Etling, "Christ Has No Body on Earth but
Yours," *National Catholic Reporter*, January 21, 2020, https://
www.ncronline.org/spirituality/soul-seeing/soul-seeing/christ
-has-no-body-earth-yours.
13. *Strong's Exhaustive Concordance*, s.v. "3144. martus," Bible Hub,
accessed July 22, 2024, https://biblehub.com/greek/3144.htm.
14. Pete Greig, *The Vision and the Vow: Re-Discovering Life and
Grace* (Relevant Books, 2004), 84.
15. Greig, *Vision and the Vow*, 84.

Chapter 11: Redemptive Suffering

1. Thomas Keating, *The Human Condition: Contemplation
and Transformation* (Paulist Press, 2014), archived at https://
www.invialumen.org/uploads/3/7/5/4/37541063/the_human

_condition_contemplation_and_transformation_by_father
_thomas_keating.pdf.

2. Romans 5:3–5.
3. Romans 8:14–17; 2 Corinthians 4:10; Philippians 3:8–11.
4. Genesis 6:5–6.
5. Luke 4:1–2.
6. David Benner, *Soulful Spirituality: Becoming Fully Alive and Deeply Human* (Brazos Press, 2011), 75–76.
7. For a fuller explanation see Ronald Rolheiser, *The Passion and the Cross* (Franciscan Media, 2015), 1–2.
8. Romans 5:5.
9. Nick Cave, *Faith, Hope and Carnage* (Farrar, Straus and Giroux, 2022), 58.
10. Romans 8:22–23.
11. Romans 8:26–27.
12. Phillip Yancey, "Parkinson's—The Gift I Didn't Want," *Christianity Today*, February 20, 2023, https://www.christianity today.com/ct/2023/february-web-only/philip-yancey-ct-parkinsons -diagnosis-gift-i-didnt-want.html.
13. Curt Thompson, *The Deepest Place: Suffering and the Formation of Hope* (Zondervan, 2023), 123.
14. Harold S. Kushner, *When Bad Things Happen to Good People* (Anchor, 2004), 111.
15. Revelation 21:3–4.
16. Philippians 3:10–11.
17. Kushner, *When Bad Things Happen to Good People*, 117.
18. Soong-Chan Rah gave this summary as part of a speaking engagement in 2015.

Chapter 12: The Way of Love

1. Galatians 5:22–23.
2. 1 Corinthians 12:7–11.
3. Sebastian Junger, *Tribe: On Homecoming and Belonging* (Twelve, 2016).
4. Junger, *Tribe*, 18.
5. Shigehiro Oishi and Ulrich Schimmack, "Residential Mobility, Well-Being, and Mortality," *Journal of Personality and Social*

Psychology 98, no. 6 (2010): 980–94, https://www.apa.org/pubs
/journals/releases/psp-98-6-980.pdf.

6. Carl Truman, *Strange New World*.

7. Mike Mason, *Practicing the Presence of People* (Random House, 1999), 236.

8. John 15:4.

9. *Strong's Exhaustive Concordance*, s.v. "3306. meno," Bible Hub, accessed July 23, 2024, https://biblehub.com/greek/3306.htm.

10. John Mark Comer, *Practicing the Way: Be With Jesus. Become Like Him. Do as He Did* (Waterbrook, 2024), 22.

11. Thomas Merton, *The Wisdom of the Desert: Sayings of the Desert Fathers from the Fourth Century* (New Directions, 1970), 34.

12. Galatians 5:22–23.

13. Ken Shigematsu, *God in My Everything: How an Ancient Rhythm Helps Busy People Enjoy God* (Zondervan, 2013), 180.

14. Timothy Fry, ed., *The Rule of St. Benedict in English* (Liturgical Press, 1981), 20–21.

15. Joseph Hellerman, *When the Church Was a Family: Recapturing Jesus' Vision for Authentic Christian Community* (B&H Publishing, 2009), 1.

16. Thomas à Kempis, *The Imitation of Christ*, trans. John Payne (1440; repr., Robert B. Collins, 1851), 153.

17. 1 Corinthians 14:12 ESV.

18. 1 Corinthians 13:1.

19. *Apostolic Faith* (June–September 1907), 2; *Apostolic Faith* (May 1908), 3, archived at the Library of Congress, accessed August 14, 2024, https://www.loc.gov/item/sn90005481/.

20. Larry McMurtry, *Roads: Driving America's Great Highways* (Simon & Schuster, 2001), 189, quoted in Leighton Ford, *The Attentive Life: Discerning God's Presence in All Things* (IVP, 2014), 111.

21. Eugene Peterson, *Practice Resurrection: A Conversation on Growing Up in Christ* (Eerdmans Publishing Company, 2010), 29.

Epilogue: The One Called Alongside to Help

1. John 14:18.

2. Matthew 8:27.

3. 2 Peter 1:21.

ABOUT THE AUTHOR

TYLER STATON is the lead pastor of Bridgetown Church. He is passionate about pursuing prayer and relationship in the honest realities of day-to-day life. Tyler is the author of two other books: *Praying Like Monks, Living Like Fools: An Invitation to the Wonder and Mystery of Prayer* and *Searching for Enough: The High-Wire Walk Between Doubt and Faith*. He lives in Portland, Oregon, with his wife, Kirsten, and their sons, Hank, Simon, and Amos.

Also available wherever books are sold

Connect with Tyler at TylerStaton.com